Sweet & Wholesome Water

*Five centuries of history of
Water-bearers in the City of London*

Ted Flaxman & Ted Jackson

Past Masters of the Water Conservators Company

2004

First published in Great Britain 2004 by
E W Flaxman,
The Old School, Cottisford,
Oxfordshire, NN13 5SW

Copyright © E W Flaxman and E W Jackson 2004

ISBN 0-9548986-0-5

Maps and plans by Colin Smith, Texprep, Brackley
Printed and bound in Great Britain by Alden Colour

Orders to:
E W Jackson, Wall Garden House, Tehidy Park, Tehidy, Camborne, Cornwall, TR14 0TN

Illustrations

The publishers gratefully acknowledge permission to reproduce the following illustrations

Copyright © the British Museum; pp 22, 24, 27, 33 (upper) and two on p 91

The British Library; p 57

Courtesy of the Museum of London; pp 33 (lower), 36, 37, 49 and two on p 45

Corporation of London Record Office; pp 20 (City Cash 1/3 fo 34), 59 (Rep 99 (1) folio 529), 61 (City Cash 2/36 fo 49), 71 (Rep 13 fo 63b) and 97 (Misc MSS/152/4)

Guildhall Library; pp 12, 16, 28, 30, 34, 44, 48 and 90 and two on p 38

By courtesy of the Trustees of the Sir John Soane Museum; p 40 (upper)

The background map to those on pp 26, 88 and 98 is reproduced by kind permission of the Trustees of the Institute for Heraldic and Genealogical Studies, Canterbury

The University of Edinburgh; p 2

Contents

Dedication

In appreciative memory of Dick – Lord Nugent of Guildford (1907–1994) – who was a staunch friend of the UK water industry for many years.

Preface

Researching and writing this short history of the Water-bearers in the City of London has been a salutary experience. Because water is conveniently available on tap throughout the City today – even in washrooms at the top of the tallest buildings – it is all too easy to forget that it was not always thus.

Today's piped water distribution network is the product of the last two centuries, at most: in the long history of the City of London it is a relatively recent innovation. For at least five centuries previously the vital task of water distribution was largely a manual job. This involved not only housewives and servants with pots and pans but also full-time Water-bearers carrying heavy loads of water in tankards through the City's streets or, in some cases, conveying it in buckets or on horse-drawn carts.

Towards the end of the 15th Century these Water-bearers formed themselves into a Fraternity. Their trade being essentially manual, they never became a Livery Company but they were nevertheless a significant organisation that represented and regulated the operation of Water-bearers in the City for well over 200 years.

The picture that emerges from our researches is utterly different from life today – more basic, more boisterous, and at times more violent. The Water-bearers evidently made only the barest of livings from a trade which must have been physically demanding. But their services were essential to the life of the City, even the poorest of households needing water at least for drinking, cooking and the washing of food. That there was a strong demand for their services is shown by the fact that during the 17th Century the Fraternity almost certainly numbered upwards of 500 members. The motto of the present-day Company of Water Conservators – "No life without water" – was as true then as it is today.

This picture of a blind water bearer appeared in an "Album Amicorum"ie a sort of autograph book prepared by a Dutchman, Michael Van Meer, while he was in this country between 1614 and 1630. A caption in old Dutch can be translated as "In this way the poor people of London carry the conduit water into the citizen's homes: as many as 4,000 people earn a living in this way".

Chapter 1
EARLY BACKGROUND

Water supplies

The Water-bearers obtained their supplies from many different sources in addition to the River Thames. In order to understand their role it is necessary first to review briefly the various sources available to them.

Both the Roman city and the Norman city (during its early years) were apparently able to obtain sufficient supplies from the River Thames, its tributaries the Fleet and Walbrook, and from numerous springs and wells in the City[1]. But as the population grew, and commerce flourished, the demand for water increased and eventually outgrew these resources. The first external supply to the City appears to have been an aqueduct begun in 1237 at the request of King Henry III to convey water by gravity from Tyburn (near present-day Marble Arch) to a Conduit* in Cheap Street[2].

Thereafter, for more than three centuries, further aqueducts and Conduits were constructed for the supply of the City, some of them financed by the City authorities and others by public-spirited citizens who gave considerable sums of money, sometimes during their lifetimes and sometimes by bequests, for that purpose. These aqueducts tapped springs and streams on higher ground north and west of the City, for example in Paddington, Marylebone, Hampstead and Highbury.

The need to obtain water from further afield was reinforced by the increasingly obvious pollution of some of the local resources. The Walbrook was vaulted over[3] in 1460 to keep the rubbish out and the Fleet became grossly polluted, partly from latrines and partly from the activities of butchers and tanners[4] along its banks.

Nowadays the word "conduit" is generally reserved for pipelines or channels conveying flow. However, in this early period the single word Conduit, although sometimes referring to an aqueduct, was more frequently used to denote a public supply structure[5] which would probably be called a cistern or fountain today. To avoid confusion here the word "Conduit" starts with a capital letter whenever it refers to a supply structure.

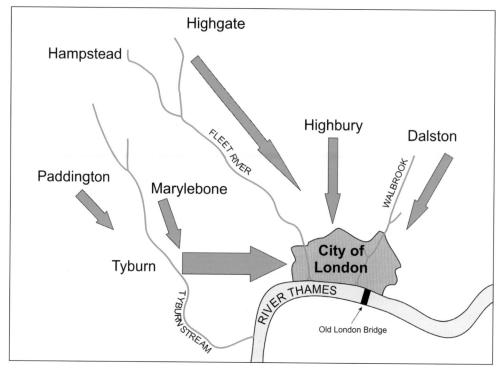

Water supplies imported to the City from higher ground to the north and west

By the time Stow came to write the first detailed account of the City at the end of the 16th century there were Conduits fed by aqueducts at more than a dozen points in the northern and central areas. Their structures were prominent features[6] of streets such as Cheapside, Cornhill, Gracechurch Street, Cripplegate, Bishopsgate, Aldermanbury, Aldgate, Holborn and Fleet Street.

Water supplied at these Conduits was free of charge to all the citizens. Those not fortunate enough to live near the river or have the use of a well were able either to take water themselves from a Conduit, to send a servant, or to pay a Water-bearer to deliver it to them.

A very small minority of citizens were sufficiently rich and influential to be able to negotiate with the Corporation for a private, piped supply to their premises. These supplies, known as "quills" were small diameter lead pipes tapped off the aqueducts. Their use frequently gave rise to widespread resentment, particularly if there was conspicuous waste in the fortunate household, or at times of a general shortage of water. The volume of water taken through quills by the privileged few was not insignificant, but their number was tiny. In the great majority of homes and workplaces, water was never plentiful, nor was it obtained without effort and/or expense.

In 1582 Peter Morice built an ingenious device utilising the power of water rushing through the narrow arches of the old London Bridge and started

*West Cheap Conduit
in olden times.*

pumping a limited supply of Thames water direct to nearby parts of the City. This supply is said to have often been turbid and foul[7], which is not surprising as, except during periods of flood tide, the intake under the northern end of the bridge was less than a mile downstream of the outlets of the grossly polluted Fleet River and the Walbrook, the discharges from which doubtless tended to hug the north bank.

Other schemes soon followed. In 1595 Bevis Bulmer[8] erected a chain pump driven by horses at Broken Wharf to supply adjacent parts of the City through lead pipes. This, too, was sited downstream of the outlet of the Fleet River and doubtless subject to the same obvious pollution.

Hugh Myddelton's New River, tapping springs from much further afield in Hertfordshire, was completed in 1613, providing a major augmentation of the supply[9]. The terminal reservoir of the New River at Islington was more than 30m above the level of the River Thames and thus capable – in theory – of supplying water under gravity to the whole of the City. But, in practice, it was more than 200 years before a fully comprehensive piped distribution system came about.

Other water companies were formed which used horse or steam power to raise water from the Thames for more general distribution through pipes. Gradually, towards the end of the 17th Century, the new piped distribution networks evidently began to impact on the trade of the Water-bearers and this competition increased throughout the 18th Century. But old habits die hard, and manual distribution of water continued for a surprisingly long period: it did not die out completely until the 19th Century.

A fatal "mischance" in 1276

The earliest reference to a Water-bearer in the City of London appears to be in a Coroner's Roll of 1276[10] describing the calamity that befell one Henry Grene in June of that year:

> *"... the said Henry, having come to St Paul's wharf with a tankard, and intending to take up water with the tankard, entered a certain boat there, and, after filling the tankard, attempted to place it upon the wharf; upon which, it so happened that, from the weight of water in the tankard, as he was standing upon the board of the boat aforesaid, the boat moved away from the wharf, and he fell between it and the quay into the water, and so by mischance was drowned ..."**

Apart from its graphic description of the accident (of a type that remains familiar to this day) this account is noteworthy in introducing the term "tankard". For hundreds of years this was the standard vessel used by Water-bearers in the City of London: it was very different from the drinking mug usually associated with the term nowadays. In a footnote to this entry in his 19th Century transcript of the Coroner's Roll, Riley gives the following useful description of the tankard used by Water-bearers:

> *"A large pail, or tub, for carrying water, was so called. The tankard contained about three gallons, was hooped round, and in figure like the frustrum of a cone: it had a small iron handle at the upper end, and being fitted with a bung, was easily carried on the shoulders".*

Many tankards were, in fact, much larger than three gallons (as will be seen from later references) but otherwise this description tallies closely with early illustrations showing tankards in use and awaiting filling at the Conduits.

Tankards had many features in common with barrels – they were circular in section, made of timber staves and held rigidly together with iron hoops. Their production was evidently a specialised form of coopering – one of the coopers named in a legal case[11] in 1298 being known as "John le Tanckardmaker".

Other early records of Water-bearers

Early surviving records of the City contain many other references to Water-

---

* *Conventional (double) inverted commas "thus" are used to denote passages copied or transcribed verbatim from the original references. Where the spelling has been modernised or the passage simplified for clarity it is contained within single inverted commas 'thus'.*

bearers. Some of these references are tantalisingly brief – merely the mention of a name. Thus, also in the month of Henry Grene's calamity, June 1276, one Osbert de Hapeneye, water-lader, was called upon[12] to vouch for a neighbour who had witnessed the accidental drowning of an unknown man whose body was lying in the "Foss under the City Wall, near the Tower". This unnamed man had apparently taken off his coat of russet and intended to bathe naked in the Foss but, "being unaware of the depth of the water, he sank to the bottom". Bathing could involve other hazards in those early years – at one time the penalty for bathing in the Thames near the Tower was loss of life and limb[13].

As in the two examples quoted above, many of these early records come from the proceedings of coroner's inquests or the courts. A few of the records are more informative, as in 1324 when Robert de St Botolph, a water bearer, was murdered in the City[14] and the jurors explained the circumstances as follows:

> *"... the said Robert and a certain "John de Parys of York" at dusk, were quarrelling in the street of "La Ryole", the said John drew his knife called "bideu" and therewith mortally struck the said Robert on the top of his head, no one else being present, inflicting a wound 3 inches long and penetrating the skull; that the said Robert thus wounded went thence to the said house of John Amyz, where he had his ecclesiastical rights, and there lingered until Saturday before the Feast of St Edmund, when he died at midnight. Being asked what became of the said "John de York" the jurors say that he returned to the house of the said William de Casis his master, and with him crossed the sea, his master not knowing anything of the felony ...".*

This is a nasty example of lawlessness in those early times, when serious arguments might be settled with the dagger. There is no mention of any attempt to apprehend the culprit – police were not to appear on the streets of London for many centuries. Neither is there any mention of medical attention for the wounded man.

Just as disputes between individuals were occasionally violent so too, at times, were conflicts between powerful trade and craft organisations in the City. This is vividly illustrated in Unwin's authoritative and oft-quoted history of "The Gilds and Companies of London" where he comments[15] on two such disputes. The first of these disputes, in 1268, was between the Goldsmiths and the Tailors and the second, in 1339, was between the Skinners and the Fishmongers. Both were "attended with bloodshed and followed by executions".

Another Coroner's report[16] on the death of a seven-year-old boy by the name of John le Stolere in 1338 provides a reminder of the unsanitary conditions of everyday life prevailing in the City at that time. A lad aged 12 was bringing a water-cart with a cask full of water belonging to his master along Chepe (Cheapside today):

> "... the same being drawn by two horses, when a wheel of the cart crushed the said John Stolere as he sat in the street relieving nature so that he immediately died; that the said William took fright and fled, leaving the cart, etc, but whither he went they (the jurors) know not ..."

In 1381, after the suppression of Wat Tyler's rebellion, a list was drawn up for the City authorities[17] giving the:

> "Names of divers men who were suspected of consenting with the men of Kent and Essex to rise against the King and kingdom, and who were of ill fame, and by reason of the said insurrection withdrew from the City of London and suburbs ..."

This list included men from a wide range of specialities including "Ralph Waterleder" from Cornhill Ward and "Richard Waterberere" from Walbrook Ward, together with sundry cordwainers, brewers, a goldsmith, joiners, weavers, tailors and so on.

Contemporary references to Water-bearers and their trade in the City's records during these years give no hint of their having established any form of collective organisation. In a book published in 1871 W H Overall[18] stated that a Water-bearers Company

> "... appears to have existed as early as 1276".

This statement has been copied, and in some cases expressed more affirmatively, by subsequent authors but no primary record has come to light supporting the notion that such an organisation existed at that early period. A Fraternity or Fellowship does not appear to have emerged until 220 years later.

Chapter 2
THE FELLOWSHIP OF
THE BROTHERHOOD
OF ST CHRISTOPHER

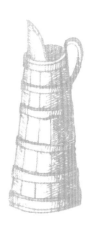

The Fellowship is formed in 1496

The later years of the 15th Century saw considerable activity by organisations in the City, several of the established Companies advancing their cause by obtaining Charters. These included the Dyers[19], Musicians[20], Pewterers[21], Carpenters[22], Cooks[23] and Wax Chandlers[24]. In the autumn of 1496 a new grouping appeared when 38 Water-bearers submitted to the Commissary of London for approval a document setting out the draft:

> *"Rules, Ordenaunces and Statutes made by the Rulers, Wardens and the hoole Felliship of the Brotherhed of Saint Christofer of the Waterberers of the Citie of London, founded and ordeyned in the Frere Augustinys of London".*

This document[25], the original of which is in the Guildhall Library, contains many features of interest and a complete transcript is included at Appendix A. The sections have been numbered in this transcript to facilitate references below.

The first point of interest is that the document was submitted to an ecclesiastical authority – the Commissary, an officer of the Bishop – not to the City Corporation. In his history of the Gilds and Companies[26] Unwin draws a sharp distinction between – on the one hand – measures devised for the practical control of trades and crafts and – on the other – the fraternal aspects of association. Because of the suspicion with which any form of association for social or political purposes was viewed by those in authority at the time, Unwin concluded that "the fraternity under the protection of the Church was the only practicable form in the Middle Ages"[27].

By 1496 these distinctions were less compelling than in earlier times and the terms of the draft document contain a mixture of provisions and controls, which can be broadly classified under three headings:

(a) social; (b) secular – in control of trade; (c) religious.

The first of these three groups included:

(i) The Fellowship was not exclusively male, It comprised both "brothers and sisters" (Paras 2, 3, 4, etc) though, in fact, all of the 38 Water-bearers named in the document as originating the Fellowship were male;

(ii) Governance of the Fellowship was "strictly oligarchical"[28] with the Wardens being chosen only by those who had previously held that post (Para 1);

(iii) Members could not arrest another member without the licence of present and previous Wardens (Para 2);

(iv) Present and previous Wardens were required to support each other (Paras 6 & 7);

(v) A prohibition on reviling any of the present or past Wardens (Para 4);

(vi) A requirement of confidentiality (Para 11);

(vii) Fines on any members of the Fellowship could be mitigated if those individuals happened to be "...of such poverty or insufficientness..." (Para 13).

The second of these groups included:

(i) A prohibition on poaching customers from other members of the Fellowship (Para 10)

(ii) A requirement to present to the Wardens within three days any non-member of the Fellowship taken into employment (Para 12)

(iii) A prohibition on any member having more than one tankard at the Conduit at any one time (Para 16 – apparently a late addition to the Ordinances).

The third of these groups included:

(i) Provision for religious observance when a member died within the City of London – torches and tapers being lit, provided that the deceased had done their duty to the Fraternity (Para 5);

(ii) Provision also for masses, torches and tapers when a member died outside the City, again provided that the deceased had done their duty to the Fraternity (Para 8);

(iii) Fines imposed on members who failed to attend the burial of a member dying within the City of London if warned to do so (Para 9).

(iv) Although some offences, such as disobeying the Ordinances (Para 3), were punishable by Fines of money (usually 6s 8d or 3s 4d), most other offences resulted in Fines payable in wax, the quantity varying from 1lb to 5 lb. For one of these offences – reviling a Warden (Para 4) – women were subject to a fine of 2 lb of wax whereas men were subject to a fine of double that quantity, 4 lb of wax. (The provision of wax for torches and tapers used in religious observance was a common feature of many Livery Companies at this time)

(v) The Commissary laid down that the rulers, wardens and brethren were to obey, observe and keep all the rules, ordinances and statutes "... undre payne of the grete curse ...". This "great curse" was Excommunication – the church's direst threat.

Three general comments can be made about these Ordinances. First, they did not include any provision for a Court of Assistants. Many of the Livery Companies were introducing around that time a Court of Assistants which was, indeed, a court with judicial powers over members[29]. That was not the case initially with the Water-bearers, the entire management of the Fellowship resting with the Wardens (past and present) who were responsible for discipline. Secondly, the individuals who were named in the preamble to the Commissary's ruling on the application comprised 3 current "rulers and wardens" and another 35 Water-bearers and they were said to be "alle or the more parte or the greter parte of the Fraternity aforesaid" implying that there were not many more members of the Fraternity at that time. Thirdly, it was usual at this time for such organisations to have a Patron Saint, and a link with St Christopher is mentioned in the preamble. He was presumably chosen

Tittle tattle at the conduit.

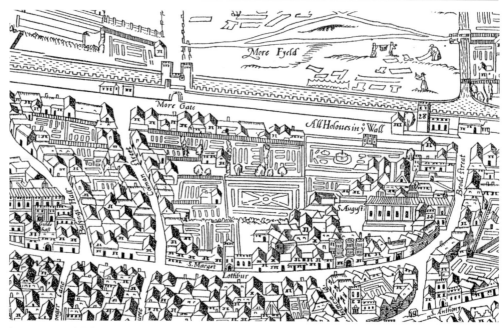

because of his association with water, having traditionally carried the young Jesus across a stream.

The Priory of Austin Friars, with whom the Fraternity was closely linked, had been founded[30] in 1253 on a site inside London Wall to the west of Throgmorton Street donated by Humphrey de Bohun, Constable of England, after his return from a Crusade[31]. The priory church had a notably tall, thin spire and was said to be "one of the beautifullest and rarest spectacles of the City": it contained the tombs of several Plantagenets[32]. Following Henry VIII's break with Rome in 1534 the Priory was dissolved in 1538. The present Austin Friars Square is on the site of the former Cloisters.

In trouble with the Authorities

No records kept by the Fraternity of Water-bearers appear to have survived, but references to their organisation are to be found in several other classes of document over the next two centuries and more. The first 40 or 50 years of the Fraternity's existence appear to have been relatively uneventful, and certainly seem not to have involved any serious difficulties with the City Corporation. But in 1547 the Court of Aldermen[33] instructed the Chamberlain to "call in to his hands the book of Ordinances made by the Water-bearers for examination". This was the opening salvo in a conflict which was to drag on for fifteen years.

By 1553 the Court of Aldermen[34] had evidently lost patience and decreed that the "Fraternity or Brotherhood of the Water-bearers" was forthwith to be "taken away, dissolved and cease". At the same time as they dissolved the

Fraternity, the Court of Aldermen instructed the Chamberlain to allow such individuals to bear water henceforth who were identified 'by their good and honest demeanour at the Conduits and otherwise towards the Citizens of this City'.

This reference to 'good and honest demeanour at the Conduits' perhaps gives a clue as to one of the reasons for the Aldermen's seemingly harsh ruling suppressing the Fraternity. Conflicts were evidently quite frequent amongst those who were waiting to fill their vessels, and in 1541 the Court had issued a proclamation against persons resorting to the Conduits with clubs and staves[35]. As the service provided by the Water-bearers was important to the life of the City, the Chamberlain was given authority to continue them in operation individually after their Fraternity had been abolished. The Court of Aldermen approved the admission of several new Water-bearers in later years[36].

The wider political background no doubt had its effect on the relationship between the Fraternity and the City Authorities. No relevant documents of Austin Friars survived the dissolution[37] but it seems likely that the elimination of the religious house with which the Fraternity had been closely associated must have weakened their position in the ceaseless struggle for power between Crown, Church, Parliament, the City Corporation and the trade guilds, which ebbed and flowed for centuries.

In a chapter devoted to the Guilds of Transport in the City – Carmen, Water-bearers, Billingsgate Porters, Watermen, etc – Unwin[38] comments that

> *"... they were recognised as fellowships by the city though they remained more under the oversight of civic authorities than the corresponding fellowships of craftsmen."*

And in discussing a brotherhood of labourers serving the building trades[39] during the 16th Century he says it,

> *"... like other of the poorer fraternities, seems to have suffered temporary eclipse during the Reformation period."*

The dispute between the City and the Fraternity continued for another nine long years. The Water-bearers submitted petitions[40] in both 1554 and 1555 to[41] be administered once more as a Fraternity, but both of these petitions were unsuccessful. In 1556 the Court of Aldermen[42] added two Articles to the Fraternity's Ordinances. But the reformation of the Water-bearers was considered again[43] in 1560 and 1561 and[44] their "misdemeanours" examined by a Committee. The matter was not finally settled until 1562, when a

Committee[45] comprised of two Aldermen, a salter and a clothworker considered the "Acts and Ordinances concerning the common Water-bearers in this city" and the Court of Aldermen pronounced the document to be "ratified, confirmed and allowed".

Details of this new set of Ordinances have not been discovered, but the two Articles incorporated in 1556 were certainly of a different character from anything included in the original document of 1496. The first of these two Articles relates to the replacement of a brother or sister of the fraternity visited with sickness or "fallen into great age whereby he or she shall not be able to carry water". The second prohibits members from storing Conduit water in their houses in "kilderkins, tubs, hogsheads, etc in order to make a scarcity". A practical restriction, evidently intended to limit hoarding and profiteering by Water-bearers during periods of water shortage.

Internal squabbles

After the new Ordinances of the Water-bearers had been approved by the City authorities in 1562, only seven more years elapsed before the Fraternity became "engulfed by internal disputes between freemen and non-freemen"[46] which had to be referred to the City Chamberlain.

This dispute appears to have originated from the Fraternity's attempt to discipline those Water-bearers who were not freemen of the City, while at the same time denying them any role in the Fraternity's internal governance. These outsiders were generally known as "foreigners". Unwin explains[47] that people from overseas were then known as "aliens", and the term "foreigners" was used to describe "immigrants from the country" ie people from Hertfordshire, Essex, Kent, Surrey, Middlesex or more distant counties. He also notes[48] that records from the reigns of Elizabeth, James I and Charles I are full of disputes arising "...between the craftsmen of the City and those of the suburbs".

The outcome of this internal dispute was a detailed ruling by the City Chamberlain[49] in September 1569 which referred to most of the freemen Water-bearers in unflattering terms as being "of the greatest disorder, simplest of discretion and most troublesome and so least meet to govern". To remedy this, the Chamberlain would himself appoint three freemen Rulers and one foreign Ruler for the next year, and thereafter the Rulers were to be elected by all the assistants of the Company.

The result was that for many years the Fraternity admitted a proportion of "foreigners" (ie non-freemen) into their number each year. This does not appear to have caused any major problems. Indeed, it may have been welcome to the Rulers of the Fraternity as they were permitted[50] to charge foreigners twice as much for admission as they charged freemen ie 2s-0d instead of 12d.

But the admission and employment of foreigners by the Water-bearers always remained under the close control of the City authorities. In 1599 the Court of Aldermen ordered[51] a general prohibition on foreigners for three years. This order does not appear to have been renewed, and such records as survive for the first part of the 17th Century show that about a quarter of new admissions to the Fraternity in each year were foreigners. Then, in 1638, the[52] City forbade the Rulers to admit any further foreigners into the Fraternity – and the practice soon died out.

About this time there was also a further internal dispute[53]. By now the Fraternity had Assistants as well as Rulers: the dispute arose between them and the Freemen members. The origins of this dispute are not clear, but the City issued a noteworthy edict[54] laying down that "two of the Rulers of the Society of Waterbearers London who are ancientest in place shall yearly hereafter be removed by the Chamberlain and two other honest and discrete persons by him chosen in their places".

This provision for an annual cull of the oldest Rulers suggests that part of the problem may have originated from some of the former Rulers continuing in office too long. At all events, this dispute did not stem the continuous flow of new recruits into the Fraternity.

The Water-bearers' Hall

One of the most intriguing documents referring to the Water-bearers is recorded as having been in the Parish Chest of St Michael's Cornhill – the present Worshipful Company's church.

A 19th Century transcript[55] of the documents in the "Great barred Chest in the Vestry" under date of 8th February 1582 included "six pieces of evidences, two obligations and a quittance concerning the house some time the Waterbearers Hall ...given by Robert Donkyn to the parish".

Robert Donkyn had been a Merchant Taylor and by Will[56] made shortly before his death in 1570 he left to the parson and churchwardens of the said parish church, for ever, the messuage or house which he had purchased on 9th October 1568 of the Company of Water-bearers of London. The property was then rented out at £4 a year and he instructed that out of the profits "one dozen of penny bread" was to be given every week "to and amongst the poorest householders of the said parish where most need shall appear, and 2 shillings of the rest of the rent I give to the churchwardens for their pains".

The provisions of Robert Donkyn's Will resurfaced three centuries later in 1870 when the Charity Commissioners, backed by the Attorney General, challenged the way in which the Merchant Taylors Company were dealing with surplus funds arising from other provisions of his Will. The case did not add anything to our knowledge of the house which Robert Donkyn had bought from the Water-bearers, but it was stated about this time[57] that it had been located at Nos 143 and 144 Bishopsgate Street Without, between Lamb Alley and Angel Alley.

Both Lamb Alley and Angel Alley were erased when the approaches to Liverpool Street station were constructed in 1873–74: more than 450 tenements[58] which had sheltered 7000 people were removed at that time including, no doubt, the site of the former Water-bearers Hall. When Stow[59] was writing about this area 30 years after the Hall had been sold he described it as somewhat unsavoury – crowded, lawless and unhealthy – though there were also respectable tradesmen such as bakers in the vicinity. The Hall had been near to the original Bethlehem Hospital (Bedlam).

It is not possible today to find any trace of this neighbourhood. However, the accompanying early map (below) dating from just before 1560 shows that the surroundings were still largely rural at that time.

An interesting fact that emerges from detailed study of the City Chamberlain's edict[60] of 1569 is that the sale in the previous year of the "Hall" in Bishopsgate Without had raised for the Fraternity no less than £35. This was a large sum at that time for such a modest organisation, though the reference to the building in the same document as a "house" should dispel any notion that

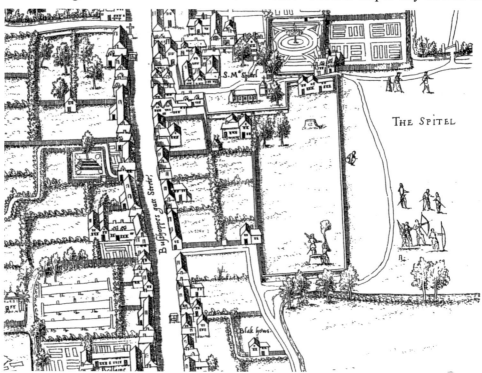

Bishopsgate Without from the oldest copperplate map of London c1559.

it was anything very grand. Indeed, in 1590, only twenty years after the premises had been bequeathed to St Michael's Cornhill two of the Churchwardens were instructed to view the house "now in ruyn and abused" and to decide whether it should be repaired or sold.

Status and discipline

Unwin[61] refers to the Water-bearers rather disparagingly as "the poorest class of labourers" and even "the despised waterbearers" There can be no disputing the fact that their trade was primarily manual, involving strength rather than skill, and they never aspired[62] to a Coat of Arms. The absence of any reference to apprenticeship in their Ordinances or other documents may be significant: not much training can surely have been needed for carrying out the job.

But they were certainly not always despised by their customers – they sometimes benefited under the Wills of well-to-do citizens[63]. Perhaps it was just that they earned so little – as implied by such descriptions as "the poore Water-Tankard bearers" which appears frequently, including in a Petition of their own to Parliament[64] in about 1621.

The relatively humble place of the Water-bearer in society was clearly depicted by Ben Jonson in his play "Every Man In His Humour", first performed in 1598 with William Shakespeare among the cast. This play is set in a small area of the north-central part of the City, between London Wall and Poultry, streets mentioned including Coleman Street, Old Jewry and Moorgate. The characters in the play include Oliver Cob, a Water-bearer, and his wife Tib who provide lodgings for a charlatan soldier in their home, which one of the other characters describes as "a base, obscure place"[65]: there is a mention of Cob's tankard. His role is not central to the main plot – which depends on innumerable disguises, impersonations and misunderstandings – but his lowly origins are clearly in evidence. In a modern commentary[66], Cob is described as a "comic lower-class character".

In the Ordinances originally submitted by the Water-bearers in 1496 they referred to themselves variously as a "Fellowship", a "Brotherhood" and a "Fraternity". Over the years the last of these terms – Fraternity – was used most commonly, but they were also described occasionally, even in City documents, as a "Company" and a "society". Clearly, not much significance was attached in those days to the exact title used for the organisation. The title "Fraternity" has generally been adopted here, except where one of the alternatives was used in an original document

Internal discipline continued to be maintained by the Rulers within the Fraternity after their enforced reformation by the City in 1562. Although it is not known exactly what penalties were introduced under the new Ordinances they were probably entirely financial. It is unlikely that penalties in wax were continued – the previous emphasis on continuing prayers for the dead having been swept away by the Reformation and its aftermath.

The City's records show that cash fines for contravention of the new Ordinances were regularly imposed by the Fraternity on members over many years – at least from 1566 to 1684. The total amounts of these fines were not trivial, amounting generally to between 5s-0d and 10s-0d in each year, equivalent to the admission of five to ten Freemen into the Fraternity. (The totals of fines in the years 1632–1650 are shown in Appendix D).

In his account of the "Government of the Companies" Unwin[67] comments that:

"The Court books of most companies began to be kept about the middle of the 16th Century, and there are very few aspects of the life of the citizen of that period that are not reflected in their records. Omitting (certain) formal items ... perhaps the most constantly recurring class of item is the record of disputes settled amongst members. Very often these have arisen out of hard words and insulting gestures ... Sometimes ... a master is imprisoned for unlawfully breaking an apprentice's head".

As no records of the Fellowship of St Christopher appear to have survived it is not possible to quote any such examples directly, but a personal dispute involving members of the Fraternity was aired in the Consistory Court of London in 1591. It appears[68] that a week before Christmas in that year one Dorothy Stockdale made "angry speeches" against a Water-bearer by the name of Robert Bridges. She repeated her accusations a fortnight later, in a "skowling manner" using the very same words again to the effect that Robert Bridges:

" ... hast had the use of four women beside hodgkins wife ..."

At a later hearing[69], when these accusations were repeated, one of the deponents expressed the view that if Robert Bridges "were such a man he was not fit to be of their company" and then another Ruler of the Water-bearers, said that "he and the rest of his fellow rulers had put the said Bridges out of their house forcibly".

This single lurid case involving a Water-bearer should not be allowed to give the impression that the Water-bearers were unusually blameworthy in this respect. An index[70] of the cases heard in the London Court during a period of 25 years from 1586 to 1611 shows the reverse. Out of the many hundreds of cases heard during this period there were only three others involving Water-bearers, and then only as witnesses.

The case involving Robert Bridges[71] is useful today because it provides one other piece of factual information about the Fraternity – that in 1591 the Water-bearers were in the habit of meeting at a house in Whitecross Street without Cripplegate. This is in the same northern area of the City as St Augustines Friars (known as Austin Friars today) and not far distant from the site of the Water-bearers original Hall in Bishopsgate Without. It was presumably from this house that Robert Bridges was forcibly ejected.

The Fraternity flourishes – 1562 to 1666

Despite being strictly supervised by the Chamberlain following their dissolution from 1553 to 1562, the Fraternity flourished, at least in terms of numbers of members, over the next hundred years or so. The most striking evidence of this is in the preamble to the Petition to Parliament from the Water-bearers in about 1621[72] which contained the phrase:

> "... from the whole company of the poore water tankard-bearers of the City of London and suburbs thereof, they and their families being 4,000 in number, living and relieved thereby ..."

The number 4,000 seems, at first sight, remarkably large, even though it specifically included families. Assuming that each Water-bearer had a wife or husband and five or six children it implies a membership of at least 500 in the suburbs and the City. It might be dismissed as a fiction, exaggerated purely in order to bolster the case being put before Parliament, were it not for two pieces of supporting evidence.

The first of these is the inclusion of precisely the same figure of 4,000 in the caption written in Dutch by Van Meer on his picture of the blind Water-bearer. (In this way the poor people of London carry the Conduit water into the citizens homes: as many as 4000 people earn a living in this way.) That might, perhaps, also be dismissed as a fiction current at that particular time, but firm evidence is to be found in the City's cash accounts.

One of the City's requirements from 1562 onwards was evidently that a moiety (ie half) of all admission fees and fines raised by the Fraternity was to be paid over to the City. Though doubtless unwelcome to the Fraternity at the time, this provision is useful today because the Corporation's surviving cash accounts reveal a great deal about the way in which the Fraternity progressed over a long period of years.

The City's accounts for 1585 show[73] that in that year 20 new Water-bearers entered the Fraternity, 13 freemen and 7 foreigners, for which the rulers paid the city a moiety of £2-9s-0½d. For the previous year[74] their payment had

City's cash book entry of 1638.

"Receaved of the Rulers of the Waterbearers for the Citties' Moiety of Lii x^s this yeare for the admission of xxviii freemen and eight forreyners into their fraternity and for fines levied upon offenders in their said fraternity this yeare   xxv^s"

been £2-18s-8½d i.e. 20% greater. There is also a fragment of a draft account for the three years 1561–63 which shows £5-2-0d being paid[75] to the City in respect of three consecutive years, which implies an annual intake of at least a dozen new members.

More detailed cash accounts for the City survive from 1632 onwards[76]. Payments by the Water-bearers and the numbers of admissions to the Fraternity recorded from 1632 to 1650 are tabulated in Appendix D. There were quite wide fluctuations from year to year in the number of admissions, but they continued at a relatively high level throughout this period – totalling 441 in 19 years. These figures, based as they are on cash payments made to the Chamberlain, are most unlikely to have been exaggerated. They provide firm evidence that the Fraternity comprised many hundreds of members over this period.

From 1650 onwards the number of admissions to the Fraternity began to diminish, varying from 8 to 21 annually during the next decade and concluding with a series of seven consecutive years – 1660 to 1666 – in which the figure of twelve admissions and the total amount of the fines remained identical at 6s 0d, year after year. By now the amounts being paid over to the City were tiny by comparison with many other receipts, and these figures seem likely to have been more notional than real – but they still indicate a continuing inflow of new members.

Over the 105 years from 1562 to 1666 average admissions of at least 15, and more likely of 20, new members into the Fraternity each year seem likely. Although life expectancy was – by today's standards – relatively short, those who survived childhood probably had working lives of 20 to 30 years. These figures again support the view that the Fraternity numbered at least 500 members during this period.

Chapter 3
THE WATER-BEARER'S TRADE

Operation

Many of the surviving records show that the Water-bearers did not usually hawk their commodity around seeking sales by chance. They generally had regular customers in quite small areas. In some cases, they became established almost as household servants of well-to-do families. When a wealthy goldsmith died in 1576 he directed that four Water-bearers should bear his corpse to the earth, one of them being referred to as 'my owne water bearer'[77].

The 1496 Ordinance[78] penalising any brother or sister taking a customer out of the hands of another Water-bearer is clear evidence of their having provided a regular service. And in Ben Jonson's play[79] written in 1598 the Water-bearer, Cob, refers to a merchant's house in Old Jewry "where I serve water".

Each Water-bearer generally obtained water from one particular Conduit. At a local level, in the Parish of St Martin's Ludgate the vestrymen laid down[80], towards the end of the 16th Century, that water was to be distributed in that Parish by three named Water-bearers and that they were to obtain water only from the Conduit at Old Bailey. They would lose their positions if they carried water outside the Parish.

In 1601 the Court of Aldermen, in an edict about the Conduits[81], referred to "the Rulers of ye waterbearers of the same Conduits". Later, in 1680, the Court of Common Council[82] required that all Tankard Bearers were to:

> "... weare a plate of pewter marked with the sign of the Conduit
> whereat they ply and the Citty arms over it ..."

The Water-bearers using a particular Conduit sometimes had some form of shelter or refuge nearby[83]. In 1648/49 "the poore water bearers of London" petitioned the City to erect a room in Aldgate Conduit yard on some void ground. After the site had been viewed by a small committee, including an Alderman, permission was granted: but the site was already very crowded and in order "not to be prejudicial either to the City or any other person" it was

A Tankard bearer of Henry VIII's time.

decreed that the room, about twelve feet square and eight feet in height, was to be: "... sett upon pillars nine or tenne foote high from the ground ..." rather in the manner of some modern construction site offices in the City, though perhaps more precarious. The modest size of this room suggests that it was intended for use by the local Water-bearers – not by the Fraternity as a whole.

The Coroner's report on the death of Water-bearer Henry Green in 1276 demonstrates the use of the Thames also as a source of water. In the earliest years the City authorities took firm action[84] to ensure that the general public had free access to the River, sometimes ordering lanes and "stairs" to be opened up when neighbouring property owners attempted to take them over for private use. As the Conduits became available in increasing numbers they offered an alternative source of free supply which was often more convenient, both from the viewpoint of location and elevation. These factors, plus the increasingly obvious pollution of the Thames along the north bank meant that the river must gradually have become less important as a source for the Water-bearers.

Equipment

The standard vessel used by the Water-bearers was the "tankard" which has already been described and is well illustrated opposite. In Ralph Treswell's celebrated "map" of Cheapside in 1585 (overleaf) there are no fewer than 14 tankards standing around the "Little Conduit" in the centre of the picture. In many cases, as in the Petition to Parliament of the early 17th Century[85] mentioned previously the Water-bearers referred to themselves collectively as "water tankard-bearers".

The Chamberlain's ruling[86] on the internal dispute in 1569 included stringent requirements concerning the Water-bearers' tankards. After stating that freemen Water-bearers were each permitted to have two tankards, it then provided that every tankard was to contain "six gallons at the least" and that "all tankards were to be surveyed, those that were lawful being marked with an iron with a sword and a 'C', and the rest broken and defaced".

Rather surprisingly, a later edict[87] from the City authorities (in 1680) specified a much smaller size of tankard – "... three Gallons and a pottle of Winchester measure at the least." ie a minimum of 3½ gallons. In this case it was laid down that all tankards were to be taken to the Guildhall so that their capacities could be "sealed" by the Hall keeper (for which service he was authorised to charge 4d).

Clearly these were important requirements, providing customers with a guarantee of quantity. Under the ruling of 1569 the specialised coopers who made the tankards presumably provided the elementary form of "hallmark" showing that they were lawful. The Cooper's Company do not have any

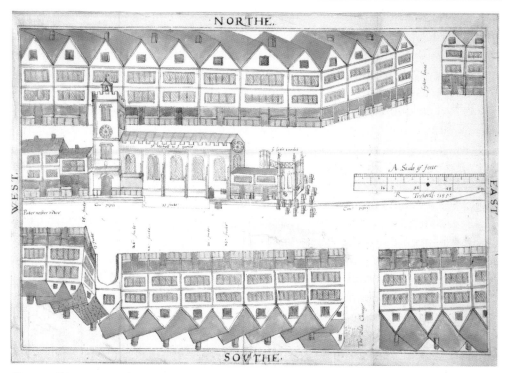

Treswell's 'map' of West Cheap showing St Michael le Quern church, the Little Conduit and 14 tankards (1585).

surviving records[88] relating to these requirements, but point out that a skilled cooper would have no problem with making a tankard of a specific capacity. Casks made for breweries are considerably more complex because of their bulbous shape, and can be made accurately to specific capacities by the small number of coopers still operating today.

In later times the Water-bearers clearly demonstrated that they were jealous of their right to use tankards. In 1630 they petitioned the Court of Aldermen[89] in protest at one of their members, by name Richard Harris, "carrying water into this Cittie in Cartes".

Although the standard vessel used by Water-bearers in the City was a tankard, a pair of buckets carried on a yoke was shown in the well-known picture[90] of 1688 in Marcellus Laroon's popular series entitled "Cries of London". A standard size of bucket would have seemed desirable if such vessels were widely used, but no such specification has been found. The puzzle of Laroon's picture is discussed further in Appendix E. Pairs of buckets on yokes are known to have been used in outlying parts of the London area, as illustrated by Barton[91] in Hampstead, and water was also sold by the pailful in Richmond at a much later date[92].

"Water-laders", "Cobs" and other names

The three terms "Water-bearers", "Tankard-bearers" and "Water-carriers" were all used to describe those employed in carrying water. These terms seem to have been synonymous and were used more or less at random. The most frequently used term was "Water-bearers", and this is the term adopted here except when quoting from a contemporary document in which one of these other two terms is used.

In the earliest years there were also a few references to "Water-laders". In a footnote to his "Memorials" of 1868 Riley[93] suggested that a "Water-lader" was the same as a "Water carrier". No clear definition of this term has come to light, but it seems probable that "Water lader" was, in fact, distinct from the other three terms and referred to carriers using containers on horse-drawn carts.

Early records of the Augustinian priory of Holy Trinity, Aldgate[94] make reference to Geoffrey le Waterlader and Robert le Waterlader, both of whom rented land in the period 1197 to 1248 – which suggests that they may have had horses. Further evidence is to be found in the Will of a "Water-lader" by the name of Geoffrey Penthogg who died in 1348 and also in the Will of his widow who died later in the same year[95]. These Wills show that they owned five horses and two carts. The most direct evidence is to be found in a set of regulations in 1350 establishing wages and prices in the City[96] which includes charges on "the carters, called waterladers" bringing their carts from the small port at Dowgate. The present-day use of the term "Bill of lading" is also indicative, the OED defining lade as meaning "load (ship)".

A further list of charges[97] payable in 1366 for bringing commodities into the City from Dowgate also included 2d per week for horses carrying bougets of water. This is the only reference to "bougets" that has come to light in these annals. They were leather containers – and also conventional heraldic emblems which appear in the Water Conservators Company's coat of Arms as shown on the back cover of this book. It seems likely that both bougets and the carriage of water on carts were replaced in the City by the fairly standard use of tankards at an early period.

In a book of 1887 by Clifford[98] it is stated that Water-bearers were sometimes known as Cobs. It has also been said that:

> *"... they resided chiefly in Cob's Court, Broadway, Blackfriars ..."*

This is thought[114] to be the same as today's small street known as Cobb's Court west of St Pauls Cathedral, just south of Ludgate Hill.

This statement about "Cobs" has been repeated in several other publications during the 20th Century. But none of the primary (contemporary) sources consulted make any mention of the term "Cob". It was used in Ben Jonson's play as a name rather than as a job description, Oliver Cob being a Water-bearer by trade, and this may possibly have given rise to the idea.

The assertion that Water-bearers "resided chiefly in Cob's Court" is also questionable. As already mentioned, each Water-bearer plied his or her trade in a relatively small part of the City, generally using just one Conduit as a source. The City's square mile comprised more than a hundred Parishes, some of them very small, within which local loyalties were strong. One would also expect the Water-bearers normally to live reasonably close to their work.

These doubts receive strong support from the Wills of Waterbearers summarised in Appendix C. Between 1363 and 1700 the Wills of 26 Water-bearers were proved in the Commissary and Archdeanery Courts of London and the Deanery of the Arches. Each of these Wills stated the Parish of the deceased and these are shown in yellow on the map below. Only one of the 26 Water-bearers lived in the Parish of St Anne Blackfriars where Cobb's Court was located. There is clearly no concentration around Cobb's Court and the notion that Water-bearers "resided chiefly in Cob's Court" seems to be a myth, generated perhaps from an imaginative misreading of Ben Jonson's play. The home of Oliver Cob in the play[99] was certainly nowhere near Cobb's Court – he lived "by the wall", almost certainly between Coleman Street and Broad Street.

Parishes of deceased Water-bearers who left Wills

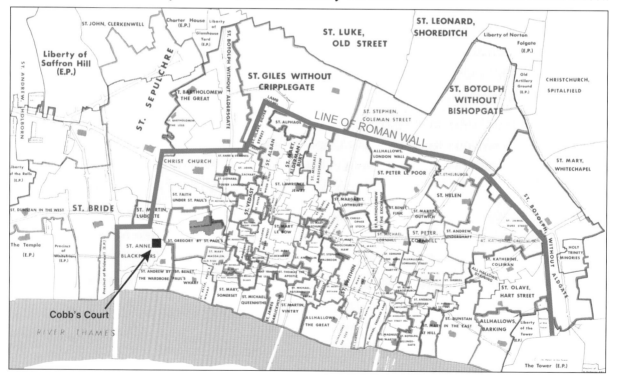

At the Conduits

Tittle-tattle or the several Branches of Gossiping

The vital importance of water in the everyday life of the City was reflected in the form and siting of the Conduits constructed as the public supply points on the various pipelines bringing water in from the north and west. These were impressive structures, large and highly decorated, often sited in the middle of major thoroughfares. There appears to have been an elevated lead tank, or cistern, into which the water flowed, with brass cocks providing outlets – sometimes at various levels – from which vessels could be filled. There are several references to the four "spouts" at the Conduit in Cornhill[100] but, by contrast, Lamb's Conduit had only a single spout[101].

The Conduits were busy, and sometimes boisterous, centres of neighbourhood life where housewives, servants and traders, as well as Water-bearers, gathered. When flows were low, or demand high, considerable waiting time must have been involved and disputes inevitably occurred. A crowded cartoon of City life known as "Tittle-tattle or the several Branches of Gossiping" which dates from the reign of Elizabeth 1st includes short pieces of doggerel about the various activities depicted, one of which reads:

"At the Conduit striving for their turn,
The Quarrel it grows great,
That up in Arms they are at last,
And one another beat,"

Marie de Medici's procession along Cheapside in 1638 showing Little Conduit (by a later artist).

Brief reference has already been made to the City's proclamation[102] of 1541 which laid down that "persons resorting to the Conduits were not to bring any clubs or staves with them" and this ruling was to be enforced on pain of imprisonment.

As early as 1338 the City[103] prescribed days on which butchers, poulterers and fishmongers might sell their goods "so as to avoid overcrowding the street between Stocks market and the Conduit in Cheap Ward". And congestion in the City streets grew worse and worse over the centuries as London grew. In 1597 Stow[104] mentioned the dangers caused by increasing numbers of cars, drays, carts and coaches in the streets and commented drily that "the world runs on wheels".

The Conduits also provided conspicuous City landmarks connected with occasions both happy and forbidding. They were often key points on the routes of major processions[105], as in 1415 on the return of Henry V after Agincourt and again in 1432 when a pageant included major items at three of the Conduits. One of these, located at the Great Conduit in Cheapside, was a pageant of Wells in honour of the Lord Mayor "embowered with a Paradise of Fruit Trees".

Occasions of great public rejoicing were sometimes celebrated by providing wine at the Conduits, instead of water. This happened when King Edward I was crowned[106] in 1273. Many years later, on the accession of King George I[107] in 1714 the Court of Aldermen decided 'to provide two hogsheads of claret for the Conduits in Stocks Market and Cheapside to run on the day of His Majesty's entrance into the City'.

In 1783, after the practice had ceased, a writer in the Gentleman's Magazine[108] commented rather disparagingly that "this method of exhilarating the common people was easy in the practice and far less expensive than would be thought because the efflux of the wine was proverbially slow, and seldom emitted a stream bigger than a straw". Nevertheless, the provision of two hogshead of claret, each of 52½ gallons, was equivalent in volume to well over 600 present-day bottles and must surely have created some exhilaration among the "common people" – at least amongst those who got there first.

A very different use for a Conduit emerged during the disturbed times of 1659–1660, immediately prior to the Restoration of the Monarchy. The City appeared to be under threat of invasion by the army because of its resolute stand for full and free Parliamentary elections and the Corporation began to organise its own militia and to set up defence lines. These defences included "great posts" set up at the Conduit in Fleet-street which were observed by Samuel Pepys on the evening of 1st January 1660 – as recorded at the start of his diary[109]. Presumably the solid stone Conduit in the middle of the street facilitated the provision of a defensive structure there.

The Conduits were also frequently the sites of public punishments. In 1583 the Court of Aldermen[110] instructed the Chamberlain to cause a post to be set up at the Conduit in Gracechurch Street 'for the whipping of lewd persons'.

In 1529 one Peter Norys[111] was imprisoned for fouling one of the Conduits and the Court of Aldermen ordered him to be stripped naked from the girdle upwards and led from Newgate to the pillory in Cornhill with a paper on his head proclaiming

"FOR A VYLLENYOUS DEDE"

Although these punishments may seem crude by present-day standards, they were a good deal less draconian than for some offences in earlier times. In 1415, John Cleydone, a currier by trade, had been tried before the Archbishop in St Pauls for having in his possession books which were judged by the Lord Mayor to be "the most perverse that he ever did read or see". A contemporary account of the trial[112] concluded with the chilling words:

"Both he and his books were burnt".

A Variety of Customers
Most of the Water-bearers" customers were doubtless householders requiring water in their homes for normal domestic uses. Drinking and cooking are two of the more obvious uses, and the washing of meat is frequently mentioned in

Effigiaut Georgius Houfnaglius Anno 1582.

Part of Hoefnaglus' 1582 picture of Nonsuch Palace, with water bearer enlarged.

contemporary records. In 1607 the house of one Robert Lee in Leadenhall Street was equipped[113] in the yard with a "wicket (ie a small door or gate) with a bolt for the Water-bearer to put water into the kitchen".

Later commentators[114] have suggested that much of the Water-bearers' business must have been with households located at a distance from any Conduit: that seems quite likely. Water makes a heavy load if carried in quantity, but many wives living close to a Conduit no doubt often had to collect the water for themselves. Certainly the Corporation's proclamation[115] of 1541 concerning the conduits made specific provision that it was 'lawful for the poor people of the City to bring to the Conduits pails, pots, pitchers and half tubs to have and carry therein their water to serve their houses only, and not otherwise'.

Regulations also governed the use to which the free Conduit water could be put. One particular problem which appears frequently in the records concerns the watering of horses. Thus in 1562 it was recorded[116] that 'Roger Jaye waterbearer was committed to prison for bearing Conduit water to a common Inn to water horses, contrary to the laws and ordinances of the City'. Horses can be thirsty creatures and it is not surprising that the City sought to reserve the free Conduit water for human use.

Use of Conduit water by various traders, particularly brewers and fishmongers, often led to problems. It was strictly forbidden at some periods and permitted under regulation at others. Thus in 1310 William Hardy[117] came before the Mayor and Aldermen to swear that he would:

"faithfully cause the Conduit in Chepe to be guarded so that brewers and fishmongers shall not use the water thereat: nor would he sell water to any one by night or day on pain of losing his freedom".

By 1415 the brewers[118] had rented "the fountains and the great upper pipe of the Great Conduit in Chepe" but were forbidden "to draw water from the small pipes below the said Conduit under penalty of paying 6s 8d to the Chamber on each conviction". Much later, in 1668, the City authorities[119] instituted a "search for water stolen or taken by brewers".

The services of Water-bearers were sometimes required for building purposes. Mark Jenner[120] draws attention to an example in 1633 during the renovation and refurbishment of a sizeable property in Blackfriars. This had recently been purchased by the Society of Apothecaries: their Archivist has kindly provided details[121] from surviving accounts showing that three substantial purchases were made from Water-bearers in February–May 1633. One of these purchases was "for Lyme" and another "for ye Plaisterers". The first was for no fewer than 215 tankards of water, and the second appears to have been for nearly 400 tankards.

The house purchased by the Apothecaries had a garden and grounds running southwards all the way to the river. In May 1633 a further quantity of water, probably amounting to about 70 tankards, was purchased by the Apothecaries from "ye Water-bearers for ye grass plot". The uses allowed for Conduit water can hardly have included garden-watering, and in this instance the Water-bearers presumably obtained their supplies from the Thames.

The Warden's accounts of the Founders Company, which have survived from 1497, provide a series of vivid snapshots of events in the life of that Company, some of them involving payments to Water-bearers. For example the expenses of a supper[122] in 1498 included "for the waterberer iiid" (ie 3d) out of a total cost of £3 – 12s – 5d. Total membership of this Company was probably less than 100, but it seems they had good appetites. Items of food purchased for the occasion included 5 dozen chickens, 30 shoulders of mutton, 10 dozen pigeons, 32 rabbits, 7 legs of mutton, large quantities of various spices as well as 2 barrels of ale and 5 gallons of wine costing 3s 4d.

Specialised employment was secured at the Church of St Mary at Hill by one Chappell, Water-bearer, who had been married[123] there in 1524. In 1528 he was paid 8d wages for the year for filling the holy water buckets in the church.

Supply problems

A fundamental problem for the Water-bearers throughout their whole long history was their lack of control over their principal sources of supply at the Conduits. The Conduits (and the aqueducts feeding them) were provided and maintained under the direct supervision of the City Corporation who appointed and paid Conduit Wardens. As early as 1325 these Wardens were provided with keys[124] and often the supply of water at a particular Conduit was limited to certain hours.

For example,[125] in 1601 the Court of Aldermen instructed the keepers of six of the Conduits that they should open them only from 5am to 11am and from 2pm to 5pm. The keepers of these Conduits, and also the Rulers of the Water-bearers, were warned that non-compliance would result in imprisonment. During periods when traders were paying fees for water from the Conduits these were sometimes collected by the keepers and some of their accounts survive at the Guildhall[126].

Over the years there are frequent references to the problems created for the Water bearers – and the public at large – by shortages in the supply of water. The growth of the City's population and the spasmodic way in which new sources were tapped caused the demand sometimes to outrun the supply. And these problems were compounded both by periodic droughts and by deliberate diversions of water out of the conduits. A few examples will illustrate the effects.

Shortages of water caused by drought

The impact of a drought in the summer of 1654 which resulted in the Conduit at St Leonards Eastcheap ceasing to run by late June was recorded by one Nehemiah Wallington[127] who lived nearby. He noted that the water bearers who used to dress up the Conduit with flowers, bows and garlands on Midsummer day, instead:

> *"hung it about with mourning cloth, with two long pieces hanging down at each end with a piece of paper written thus – "the cause of this our mourning is our exceeding want of water which formerly we have enjoyed". And there were two water-bearers, a man and a woman clothed in black, which they called my lord and lady, and they went round about the conduit with many other water-bearers after them with the tankards under their arms with the mouths of the tankards downwards in a doleful manner, saying at every corner of*

*the conduit "It is not for bread nor for beer we mourn, but we mourn
for water."*

As Wallington noted at the time, this was a serious matter for the Water-bearers
who were "like to be undone for want of work". Water did not begin to flow to
the Conduit in Gracechurch Street again until 10th October when it was "a
great cause to be thankful".

In August 1621 when supplies had evidently run low, the Rulers of the
Water-bearers petitioned the Court of Aldermen[128] for permission to pump
additional water at the Conduit head near Tyburn. This emergency measure
probably related to a "great pump of lead" shown by a City inventory[129] of 1651
to have been situated at the lower end of two meadows belonging to the City
near there. Permission was granted, but the authorities rather ungenerously ruled
that it had to be paid for by a levy on those of the Water-bearers who were not
able to take part in the pumping operation through age or debility of body.

*Left: Later
impression of
pump in
Gracechurch
Street.*

*Right: Medieval lead
water pipe.*

To the Honorable Aſſembly of the Commons Houſe of Parliament, and to the
Committie for grieuances of the ſame Houſe.

33

The humble Petition of the whole companie of the poore Water-Tankerd-bearers of the
Citie of London, and the Suburbs thereof, they and their families being 4000 in number,
liuing and releeued thereby. Robert Tardy Water-bearer in the name and behalfe of
the reſt followes this Petition.

Preamble of Petition to Parliament c 1621.

Shortages of water caused by diversions

The Petition to Parliament which has already been mentioned[130] from the "... whole companie of the poore Water-Tankerd bearers ..." quoted extensively from an Act[131] of 1543–44 under which water was to be conveyed to the City from Hampstead Heath, Hackney, Muswell Hill and other places to the north and west. Eighty years later the petitioners were complaining about breaches of provisions in the Act intended to prohibit diversion of water out of the aqueducts, reciting that:

> "notwithstanding the Act, most of the water is taken and kept from the conduits in London by many private branches ... laid into private houses and dwellings, both without and within the citty ... to the generall grievance of all good citizens ..."

No record survives of what, if anything, was done about this complaint – it does not appear to have been discussed by Parliament. The small number of individuals who negotiated "quills" from the conduits to their private houses over the years were generally in positions of great power. The "hyghe honrable Thomas Cromwell", the Lord Chancellor, was but one example – his house having been provided with a quill at his request[132] in 1537.

But complaints about such diversions, even by the great and the good, did occasionally produce results. An apologetic letter[133] written by the Lord Mayor in June 1608 to the Earl of Suffolk explained that the "clamour of the poor is such at this time of dearth and scarcity" that he was obliged to cut off some of the Quills. Having told the Earl what had been done in an attempt to relieve the shortage of water, the Lord Mayor went on to voice a criticism which appears repeatedly over the years:

> 'of the exceeding great waste of water in that house beinge taken not only for the necessary use of dressing Meate but for the Laundry for the Stable and for such other Offices as might be otherwise served'.

In 1560 when supplies[134] of water were particularly short, a group of people, including Water-bearers, resorted to desperate measures. Several of them attempted to pull up the lead pipe (quill) supplying the house of Lord Paget in Fleet Street and were arrested and committed to Newgate prison. Most of those involved were soon pardoned and released by the authorities, who may well have felt some sympathy with their complaint. The ringleader, having been recommitted to Newgate, was eventually released on condition that he did not "... hereafter bere any water as a common waterbearer upon payne of imprisonment".

In the first two decades of the 17th Century, long-standing water supplies by means of quills to the Halls of the Grocers[135] and Drapers Companies[136], and to the College of Physicians[137] were challenged by the Corporation. In the case of the Drapers the supply appears to have been cut off for several years[138]. The Physicians were more fortunate: although an order was made for their pipe to be cut off, this was soon rescinded and it was agreed that their pipe would only be "... stopped during the time that the scarcitie of water continues".

Occasionally, major losses of water also occurred through bursts on the aqueducts. For example, in 1388 there were complaints[139] from residents of Fleet Street about properties being flooded due to broken pipes carrying water to the Conduits.

Shortages of water caused by theft

Illegal connections by enterprising citizens were not easy to detect. When William Campion[140] was caught out in 1478 it was found that he had dug down to the City's pipe, broken into it, and made an unlawful connection to a well at his house in Fleet Street. Evidently determined to make an example of him, the Mayor and Aldermen ruled that he should "be taken out of the Bread Street Compter (ie prison), where he was confined, and set upon a horse with a vessel like a conduit full of water upon his head ... the same water running by small pipes out of the same vessel, and that when the water is wasted new water to be put in the same vessel again" He was to be conveyed to Leadenhall, the pillory in Cornhill, the Great Conduit in Cheap and various other points in the City, at each of which a proclamation was to be made of his misdoing. Thus anticipating by 400 years Gilbert and Sullivan's making "the punishment fit the crime". After this public shaming he was to be brought back to the Compter and would remain there at the will of the Mayor and Aldermen.

In later years, much more serious shortages of water in the City were caused by theft in the West End. In 1682 a newspaper report[141] spoke of scarcity of water at the conduits "for above two Months, so that the poor men and Women, that used to get their Bread by that Employ, are almost Starved.

The Court of Aldermen had employed men to search out where the water was conveyed, and they found that it was conveyed to St James's Soho and the rest of the new Buildings. All industry should be used to find out the Persons that have thus conveyed the Water, and Actions brought against them, at Common Law, for so doing, to the content of the Poor Tankard-Bearers".

Whether any such "Actions" were ever taken is not known. The report makes it only too plain that the increasing amount of building taking place west of the City, on formerly open ground from which much of the natural flow of water had already been diverted into the Conduits, was presenting the developers with irresistible temptations to make illegal tappings into the aqueducts which ran beneath the area.

Occasionally, loss of water was caused by theft of the valuable lead pipes themselves. In 1560, on St Andrews Day (30th November) the diarist[142] Henry Machyn recorded: "... that day was no water in any condyth in London, but in Lothbere" and two weeks later that:

> *"the xiiii day of December was two men wypyd for cuttying of pypes of lede, the wyche lettyd that we had no water on sant Androwes day last".*

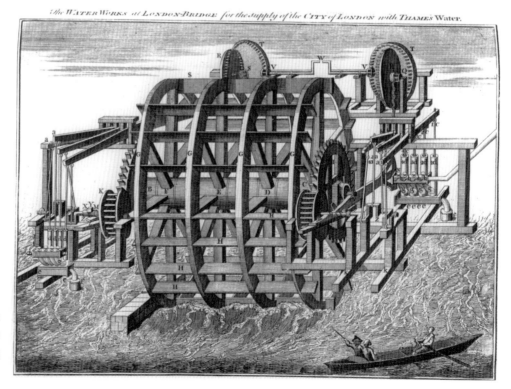

Peter Morice's waterpumps under London Bridge.

Competition

The first serious competition encountered by the Water-bearers was Peter Morice's pumping plant under London Bridge. When this was "long and largely debated" by the City in 1582 the interests of the Water-bearers were not entirely forgotten, it being recorded[143] that this would be:

> "... a good worke, very godly, very profitable for the whole Citie both ritch and pore, and no hindrance to any man namely to the poore waterbearers, whoe are neverthelesse to have as much worke as they are able to doe, so farr as the water of the Conduit will suffice, and more they never cold have ..."

This initiative, and others that followed, for bringing in additional supplies either pumped from the Thames or diverted from the higher ground immediately to the north and west, were relatively modest in scope. The amount of water they could convey being limited by: (a) the rudimentary pumping equipment available; (b) the relatively small size and pressure capabilities of the lead pipes then available.

Section through seamed lead water pipe.

Lead pipes had been known since the time of the Romans. They were generally made from seamed sheet lead until about 1539 when a method of casting was developed[144]. Apart from small diameter pipes for connections – probably less than ½ inch dia – they seem not to have been in common use, probably because of their expense in larger diameters. In 1551, when King Edward VI needed lead pipes for his own purposes the Lord Treasurer was obliged[145] to send a letter to the Lord Mayor asking 'for the borrowing of the City's mould for the casting of a great water pipe for the King's Majesty'.

Construction of the New River in the early years of the 17th Century,

Above: *Hollar's 1665 engraving of Round Pound.*
Below: *Hollar's engraving of Round Pound at Islington showing Old St Pauls in the Background (1666).*

largely on the initiative of Sir Hugh Myddelton, transformed the situation by bringing in a plentiful supply of water from further afield. The New River was more than 38 miles in length, comprising a channel about 10ft wide along which the water generally flowed about 4ft deep[146]. The fall from the springs at Amwell and Chadwell to the terminal reservoir at Islington was sufficient to convey by gravity a flow much greater than the total of all the previous imported supplies.

At the time it must have appeared to the Water-bearers that the availability of this greatly increased – and commercial – supply at an elevation commanding the whole of the City by gravity would sound a death knell to their trade. They appear to have petitioned vigorously against the scheme[147]: although these efforts failed, the New River proved in practice to be much less of a threat to their trade than anyone could have foreseen.

On its completion in 1613 the channel forming the New River was acclaimed as a triumph and there was a great ceremony attended by the Lord Mayor at its terminal, the Round Pond at Islington, to mark the occasion[148]. But for many years the project suffered a chronic weakness in the lack of an efficient and durable piped distribution system. Large volumes of water could now be brought to Islington, but conveying that water into the City and distributing it to individual properties represented an even more difficult and long-lasting challenge, which was not fully overcome for more than two centuries.

The New River Company generally used elm pipes for distribution mains, lead pipes being provided only for small diameter connections. These elm pipes were expensive[149] and not very durable: the best of them might last 20 years and the worst only 5 years[150]. To obtain suitable trees the Company had to search as far afield as Berkshire, Middlesex, Essex, Buckinghamshire and Kent[151] After the trees had been located, purchased, felled and trimmed, the trunks then had to be transported to "Pipe Borer's Wharf" in Southwark, the final part of the journey often being made by river. The pipes were generally from 3 inch to 7 inch internal diameter and primitive joints were formed by the pipes being:

> "... sharpened like pencils at one end (the top) and bored out at the other end (the butt). To effect a joint the top end of one pipe was rammed into the butt end of another".

These elm pipes were also extremely heavy and cumbersome to handle and lay. Many surviving examples show that they had wall thicknesses of up to 6 inches. The work of laying them was generally done at night, pipes up to 10ft

Above: Leaking wooden water pipes of New River Company crossing over the Fleet River.
Right: Section of ancient wooden water pipe 6" internal diameter with walls from 2" to 5½" thick

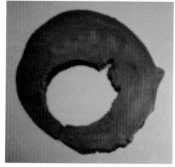

long[152] being hauled through the streets on pairs of coach wheels[153] and then lowered down into the trenches using iron chains and tarred ropes: candles illuminated the scene. Such pipes had little resemblance to the highly efficient metal or plastic pipes available for water distribution today which, for normal pressures, often have wall thicknesses of ½ inch or less.

The introduction of cast iron pipes, commenced by the Chelsea Company, from 1746 onwards[154] started a very slow improvement, but it was not until the early years of the 19th Century that improved joints for cast iron began to allow a proper pressurised distribution system to be installed. The first major

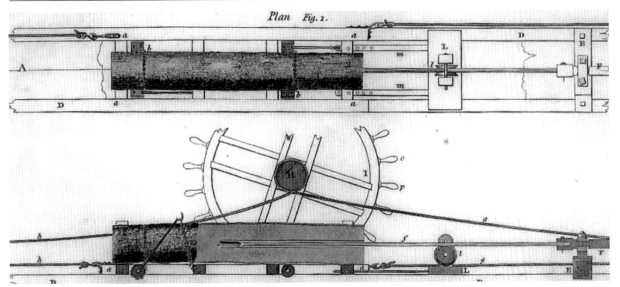

Pipe boring machine.

legislative step forward was the Metropolitan Paving Act of 1817, which prohibited the laying of timber pipes[155].

In 1778, more than 150 years after the New River supply had come into use, a street opening in Soho provided doleful evidence[156] of the state of London's underground infrastructure at that time. When a hole two feet deep was dug by workmen they "found the Water Pipes which lay across the Sewer rotten" and were ordered "to acquaint the Water Companys thereof".

Because the New River Company's distribution network suffered these serious limitations pressure was seldom great enough to reach much above ground level. The water was often discharged into basement cisterns from which it then had to be drawn. And the supply was almost invariably intermittent. In some cases, supplies were furnished to customers for a few hours on only two days a week, and one commentator remarked that the only way to obtain a better supply was to bribe the turncock[157]. Even as late as 1874, by which time the New River Company was serving over 100,000 customers, only 1% of these enjoyed a constant supply[158].

The result was that the service provided to its customers by the New River Company was – by today's standards – feeble and fitful. The limitations of this supply saved the Water-bearers from early extinction. The large numbers of members joining the Fraternity during the period 1630 to 1650, after the New River's completion, is clear evidence of that fact.

Water quality

To most of the City's inhabitants during these years, questions of water quality were probably of secondary importance. What really mattered was obtaining a regular, dependable supply at little or no cost.

Nevertheless, the taste and smell, and perhaps the turbidity of waters from the more polluted sources must, at times, have been obvious enough to those who received them. And it is said[159] that "rumours spread by resentful water-carriers" were one of the reasons for the very slow initial take-up of the supply offered by the New River Company. There was apparently a belief that piped water was unhealthier than alternative supplies from wells or the Thames, and even as late as 1700 a prejudice against New River water is apparent in a question[160] posed to a committee of the Court of Aldermen in that year. In connection with the prison at Ludgate, the committee was asked to explain:

> *"...why the Prisoners there have so often refused to accept of the New River Water till there can be a Sufficiency of Conduit Water provided for them..."*

This prejudice may not have been entirely without foundation. Particularly in the early years, when the catchment areas west of the City were still rural, it seems likely that the Conduit supplies – conveyed under positive pressure through pipes from Tyburn to the City – were of good quality. The quality of water pumped out of the Thames must certainly have been inferior because of the heavy load of pollution contributed by the Fleet River and other discharges. Contrary to what might be expected, the quality of the New River water was probably also inferior. A fuller discussion of these quality issues can be found in Appendix F.

Cost

Economic considerations must also have played a large part in the fortunes of the Water-bearers and the Water Companies with whom they were competing. Figures recorded in various contemporary accounts show that water distributed manually was, by today's standards, relatively expensive.

Although there is some variation in the prices recorded in different documents, the figures are all reasonably consistent. Towards the end of the Sixteenth Century, water-bearers in the Parish of St Martins Ludgate[161] were required to provide 7 tankards of water for two pence: other accounts refer to a penny normally being the price of three tankards. When the Society of Apothecaries[162] purchased 215 tankards of water in 1633 they paid 7s 2d, equivalent to 2½ tankards for a penny. In 1654 Nehemiah Wallington[163] noted that during the course of the drought "the price of a tankard of water had risen from a farthing to two-pence". Assuming the contents of a tankard during this period to be six gallons, as had been laid down by the City in 1562, it appears

that the volume of water purchased from a Water-bearer for a penny varied –
in normal times – between 24 and 15 gallons, and in periods of shortage might
be as little as 3 gallons.

The relatively high cost of such supplies may be judged from a present-
day comparison. Inflation during the last 350 years has caused the value of
money to diminish[164] by a factor of around 80. In terms of today's money, the
least costly of the figures quoted above is equivalent to over £4 per cu m, ie
seven times the amount currently paid by the authors for that volume of high
quality water, delivered under pressure throughout their homes.

Comparisons based solely on the overall purchasing power of money
cannot, however, provide the whole picture. The amount of disposable income
available to the purchaser is also of crucial importance. During the centuries
when Water-bearers were operating in the City of London many of the citizens
had very small incomes and preferred to make frequent payments of a few
farthings to a Water-bearer than to meet the relatively large yearly or half-
yearly charges of a Water Company (often £1 per annum) plus, in many cases,
a substantial connection charge before the supply could be commenced.

Economy in the use of water must have been strict in most households and
the quantities involved were – by today's lavish standards – miniscule. Even
the fortunate few who had a "quill" received only a limited supply. The term
"quill" is thought to have originated from the diameter of a swan or goose
quill[165] – probably about ¼ inch (6mm). When the Water-bearers complained[166]
in 1620 about the quill provided to Lady Swinnerton from the aqueduct feeding
the Conduit in Aldermanbury it was found on investigation by the Court of
Aldermen that her household had received:

> "... a greater quantity of water than her Allowance from this Court
> being two gallons of water an hour ..."

Such a tiny "allowance" as two gallons an hour would today prompt strident
complaints from the least demanding in the land, let alone from the nobility. A
typical present-day garden tap produces double that quantity in a minute.

Very different standards of water use obviously applied, even amongst the
rich. King John[167] was said to have been regarded as:

> "...rather peculiar because he had as many as eight baths in the short
> space of six months".

And, more than four Centuries later, the sophisticated diarist John Evelyn
decided, as an experiment, to try washing his hair once a year[168].

Chapter 4
DECLINE AND DISAPPEARANCE

And then – "The Great Fire"

The event which has been known ever since as "The Great Fire of London" was a disaster of such proportions that its impact on the lives of humble citizens, such as the Water-bearers, must have been catastrophic. A latter-day comparison provides some indication of its scale. During the "Blitz" in the Second World War, when London was subjected to high-explosive and incendiary bombs, aerial mines, V1 "Doodlebugs" and V2 rockets, somewhat under half of the total area of the City was laid waste in just over four years[169]. The Great Fire destroyed 436 acres – more than three quarters of the City – in four days.

London, like many provincial towns and cities, had suffered serious fires

Hollar's engraved map of the City of London showing in white the area destroyed by the Great Fire.

before. And the City authorities had issued several edicts requiring Parishes and householders to keep both equipment and stores of water in reserve. But in September 1666 several key factors conspired to encourage the flames. One of these factors was shortage of water. The summer of that year had been exceptionally hot and dry, so that both wells and supplies from the Conduits were low. By chance, Peter Morice's pumping machinery under London Bridge was temporarily out of commission: in any case it was soon consumed by the flames.

Even where water could be found, the equipment available for projecting it onto the burning buildings was woefully inadequate. Rudimentary "engines" had been available[170] since about 1625 and there were probably as many as 100

These Engins (which are ... the best) to quinch great Fires

Above: *Fire engine of 1678.*
Left: *Later impression of a 'squirt' in action.*

of these available in the City in 1666. Manually operated by a small team of men working long handles up and down, most of them produced only an intermittent jet of water from a small-diameter hand-held hose. Having little on-board storage capacity, they soon required to be replenished with water by chains of men using buckets.

The Great Twelve Livery Companies had each been instructed[171] in 1642 to obtain one of these fire engines. In 1654 the Goldsmiths Company decided to purchase a bigger "engine for the quenching of fire" and spent the considerable sum of £14 on it. At the same time the Goldsmiths arranged that 6 almsmen were to attend the fire engine at the call of the Beadle and to clean it after use, being paid for their services[172]. Despite these precautions, Goldsmiths Hall was destroyed, as were the Halls of 43 other Companies[173].

A greater number of 'squirts' was available. These were heavy brass contraptions which allowed a three-man team to project one gallon of water onto the fire at intervals. Rather like a muzzle-loading firearm, these squirts then had to be laboriously refilled with water before they could be used to project a further one gallon onto the fire.

Timber buildings were dry and readily combustible, and a strong easterly wind fanned the flames. And on top of all these physical factors, lack of proper organisation played a major part in the catastrophe. Some small groups of individuals, desperate for water, dug up the streets to get at the wooden water pipes beneath in order to sever them[174]. Because pressures were already low, the quantity of water obtained by these drastic measures proved hopelessly insufficient to arrest the fire: and two additional problems were created. Water supplies elsewhere were cut off; and access was impeded for carriers who were trying to get both into and out of the City.

Water-bearers, like many other citizens, were no doubt involved in exhausting tasks throughout the whole four days, trying to save their homes and belongings, and then participating in the combined efforts, led by the King and the Duke of York, to arrest the fire by creating breaks. The use of long "fire hooks" to pull down houses in advance of the fire[175] – a common method of fire control at the time – was employed from an early stage and eventually, when this proved fruitless, gunpowder was resorted to. But every effort to create a break, including the major corridor of the Fleet River (now Farringdon Street), on which great hopes had been pinned, proved unavailing because of the strong and continuing east wind which blew embers far ahead of the flames. Having leapt across the Fleet River the fire then swept down Fleet Street: had the wind not suddenly abated on the fourth day there seemed every prospect that Westminster would have been utterly destroyed too.

The difficulties faced by individual Water-bearers in the aftermath of the fire must have been awesome. A serious outbreak of plague in the previous year had no doubt taken its toll of them and their families and now, homeless and lacking any form of insurance for such property as they had possessed, their prospects in the autumn of 1666 were bleak. Many must have faced destitution and they (together with their families) were doubtless amongst the large numbers who "spent the cold winter of 1666-67 in makeshift shelters on Moorfields" just outside the City walls[176].

To add to the Water-bearers' troubles, most of their customers had also lost their homes and businesses, and many of their principal sources of water at the Conduits had been damaged or destroyed. In the year following the Great Fire, one Samuel Rolles published[177] a quaint series of "Meditations and Contemplations" on the "Burning of London in the year 1666" which included a Meditation upon the "spoiling of Conduits and other Aqueducts by this fire".

This referred to the stone of the Conduits not having been easy to burn down, but the fire "melting those leaden Channels in which the water had wont to be conveyed" After describing several Conduits confronting "that great enemy Fire", Rolles continued that:

> *"...As if the Fire had been angry with the poor old Tankard-bearers, both Men and Women, for propagating that Element which was contrary to it and carrying it upon their shoulders as it were in State and Triumph; it hath even destroyed their Trade, and threatened to make them perish by fire, who had wont to live by water..."*

The restoration of supplies at the Conduits was clearly of key importance to the Water-bearers if they were to continue. But it was also, unfortunately, beyond their control as it depended entirely on the City authorities.

Water supplies following "The Great Fire"

The problems created for the authorities by the Great Fire were numerous and pressing. In the previous year, the outbreak of plague had killed about a quarter of London's inhabitants[178] and now the destruction of most of the City's fabric coincided with a marine war against Holland which was not going well. Money was in very short supply and, in coping with the crisis created by the fire, the Government evidently did not regard the restoration of water supplies in the City as being high on their list of priorities.

The first Act of Parliament "For Rebuilding the City of London"[179] received the Royal Assent on 8th February 1667. It was largely concerned with re-establishing boundaries and ownership of land; introducing some pre-planning into both the street layout and the quality of the new buildings; and

Plan view of Cornhill area in 1590 showing two Conduits located in the centre of streets at junctions.

imposing a Coal Tax to help pay for the work. The only reference to the Conduits (Section XXII) merely gave the City authorities power to move them or reduce their size:

> *"... as the Freedom and Openness of the Streets conduceth much to the Advancement of Trade and Ornament of the City ..."*

Considerably more was said about the siting and sizing of sewers, drains and vaults (Section XX) and the reconstruction of Morice's Water House on London Bridge.

Following this, on 4th September 1668 (exactly two years after the fire) the Court of Common Council[180] instructed a Committee to consider how such of the Conduits as

> *"... stand in ye ruins & shall be found to be inconvenient either in respect of ye passage through ye streets or otherwise shall be wholly removed or contracted in such manner as this Court shall think fit"*

The Committee's report, dated 23rd October 1668, made detailed recommendations[181] for all the Conduits affected by the fire. These recommendations involved, as expected, either the resizing or the resiting of

Curds and Whey seller in Cheapside.

individual Conduits. Most of the Conduits were to be taken down and replaced but two, in Fleet Street and at Dowgate, were to be permanently taken away.

Several of the new Conduits or Standards were to be made either "ornamental" or "ornamental and graceful". That at St Michael le Quern Church (at the West end of Cheapside) was to be taken down and a new one erected in the centre of the three streets there meeting which was to be made "extraordinarily ornamentall" because it stood at "ye most eminent place or street for passage within this Citty".

The Committee's report made no mention of likely costs. The Court of Common Council expressed their general approval of the proposals but "… in respect of the great charge it will require to performe ye works …" suspended any work for the present other than the removal of the Conduits located in Fleet Street and Gracechurch Street.

Progress on the recommended work seems to have been slow, though supplies of water must have been restored to most areas even where the Conduit structures themselves had not been repaired. But as late as 1674, eight years after the fire, there was still one Conduit – in Aldermanbury – which remained in ruins and the Court of Aldermen directed[182] the City Plumber to:

"forthwith cause the Conduit Water to bee conveyed to the said place through a small cock for present use until the said Conduit shall be finished".

A surviving list[183] summarising the City's expenditures on Conduits and Pipes about this time shows substantial sums paid for "new building the Conduit without Cripplegate", "taking down Grace Street Conduit" and for conveyance of water and other works relating to Holborn Conduit, Cheapside, Fleet Bridge, Aldgate Conduit and the source at the Banquetting House. These expenditures totalled no less than £4,564, but removal of the Conduit structures out of some of the City's streets remained an issue.

In October 1671, the Court of Common Council[184] established yet another Committee to look again at the original proposals for removing and contracting "the Conduits of ye Citty destroyed by the late dismal fire" and to consider "what is fitt to be done in performing of the said affair" Although reminders[185] were issued in 1673 and 1675, it was not until 1680 that a report was eventually submitted. The preamble to the document[186] referred to delays in execution "for many years ... having been very prejudicall to this Citty ..." A definitive Bill based on the report was approved by the Court of Common Council and became a formal Act of that body.

This Act is reproduced in full in Appendix B. It represents an important statement of the City's intentions at that time, both in relation to the continuing provision of Conduit supplies and to the operation of the Water-bearers.

The City restated its intention (Appendix B line 90 et seq) to continue supplying water free of charge at the Conduits, at which:

"... Cittizens and Tankard-bearers to resort unto and fetch water Gratis ..."

This was exactly as before – the public supply remaining "Gratis". But a very important change was made in connection with the "quills" tapped off the aqueducts in order to supply private houses. These were now to be granted only when the Committee was satisfied that supplies to the Conduits were assured, and were also to be subject to a formal lease (Appendix B line 117 et seq) of not more than 11 years subject to a half-yearly rent. Thus, for the first time in more than four Centuries, the City authorities accepted the principle that some, at least, of the water they piped into the City was to be paid for by those who benefitted. And a further important change was that the Committee was empowered (Appendix B line 155 et seq) to agree a lease to any person of the profits arising from rents of such quill supplies.

So far as the Water-bearers were concerned, their activities were to be even more closely supervised than before. Within six months of the Act (Appendix B line 211 et seq) being passed every Water-bearer was to procure a Certificate from the Alderman or Deputy and Common Councilmen living in the same Ward to show that:

> "... they are freemen of the Citty or Widdows of freemen and persons of sober and honest conversation ..."

They were also (Appendix B line 215 et seq) to wear a pewter plate marked with the "sign of the Conduit whereat they ply and the Citty Arms over it". And their tankards were now to be sealed by the Hall-keeper (Appendix B line 204 et seq) at the Guildhall:

> "... as all other Measures are, so that the same may contain the just and full measure of three Gallons and a pottle of Winchester Measure at the least ..."

No reason has been discovered for this substantial reduction in the minimum capacity of tankards from the original figure of 6 gallons in 1569 to only 3½ gallons in 1680.

Finally, the Chamberlain was empowered (Appendix B line 220 et seq) to "heare mediate and determine all ... differences and strifes" that might arise or happen between such Tankard Bearers, with powers of both suspension and total discharge of any Tankard Bearer not conforming to such orders and rules.

An interminable fiasco

In February 1679, eighteen months before this important Act was finally approved by the City, the Court of Common Council had already given instructions[187] for one major piece of construction work – the new Conduit at the upper end of Cheapside. The intention had been expressed more than ten years earlier that this particular Conduit, when rebuilt, should be "extraordinarily ornamental" because of its key location in the City. That intention certainly appeared to have been fulfilled when the Court, having seen a "modell" of a grandiose proposal which would include an obelisk no less than 160 feet high, instructed that it be 'speedily erected". The charge was to be borne out of the "Cole Duty".

Acting with remarkable speed the City Lands Committee called for bids and, after considering several offers, let a contract[188] in March 1679 to Thomas Knight, who was described as a builder, and was also at that time the City's

Mason. The original Conduit had been badly damaged during the Great Fire and so, too, had the adjacent church of St Michael le Quern. The remains of the church had been taken down soon after the fire and the Parish united with the adjacent Parish of St Vedast, Foster Lane[189]. Construction of the proposed new Conduit was complicated by the fact that it was to be carried out partly on the site of the former church, but the builder was to receive directions for "the decent disposal of the bones at the foot of the Obelisk". The original programme required completion in the remarkably short time of 7 months.

After the Act had been passed, the Court of Common Council resolved that "for the more speedy despatch of so useful a worke" they would raise a charge of "four fifteenths", each amounting to £500. ("Fifteenths" representing a time-honoured method of raising cash by general contributions throughout the City). It was anticipated that this would also permit work on the Conduits in Aldermanbury and Lothbury.

By December 1680 the original builder, Thomas Knight, was dead[190] and the contract had been taken over by the new City Mason, Jasper Latham. The original 7-month programme had already proved to be wildly over-optimistic and work seems now to have proceeded at a snail's pace. In December 1681 an indignant petitioner by the name of Isaac Mountfort[191] sought compensation because his horse and dray had fallen into the excavation there and the Court of Aldermen[192] promptly ordered Jasper Latham to "... bring up the foundation of the said Conduit, make good the said ground and clear the said passage with all expedition ..."

Six members of the Court of Aldermen were asked "as often as their ... occasions wil permit to undertake the trouble of repairing to the said place and see that the said works be carried on with all possible despatch". In the same month it was recorded[193] that an Alderman had personally advanced money towards the building of this Conduit. But the construction work was apparently[194] still not out of the ground, and in March 1682 another of the Aldermen reported that:

> "... it will be necessary to make a vault for the Convenience of the pipe at the Conduit in Cheapside ..."

It was ordered that the vault be made accordingly, but not to cost more than £20.

More than two years later, in November 1684, money had run so short that the Court of Aldermen recorded "the inability of the Chamber of London to advance monies for the carrying on and finishing the Conduit begun to be set up with the Mayor's approbation at ye upper end of Cheapside". An appeal was sent[195] to many of the City Companies for financial contributions towards the cost. By June 1687 exasperation was beginning to set in and the Court of Aldermen instructed[196] that:

> *"... Mr Chamberlain cause the conduit at the Upper end of Cheapside (which hath never yet bin finished) to be made handsome and Ornamentall in such manner as may be done with the least expence".*

It was now eight years since the contract for the Conduit and its 160 ft obelisk had originally been let but, despite this instruction, the work seems to have effectively come to a standstill. Eleven years later, in 1698 the inhabitants[197] near the Conduit complained that the ground adjoining it "is made use of as a common laystall" ie a rubbish dump. By 1707 the area had become an unsavoury mess[198] with the laystall causing great annoyance by reason of the "stench and ill smells which arise therefrom". No water had been available there for many years and a petition from the local inhabitants concluded that:

> *"... the Conduit as it now stands is neither ornamental nor useful".*

The structure remained unfinished for many more years. It was still there in 1720 and is said[199] to have been finally pulled down in 1727.

A major construction project initially scheduled for completion in 7 months and actually unfinished after 48 years must surely constitute some sort of unenviable record.

Problems with the aqueducts supplying the Conduits

For the Water-bearers who had previously operated at the upper end of Cheapside, the City's failure to complete this landmark Conduit must have been extremely disappointing. But that was only a local problem. During the later years of the 17th Century, other parts of the intended overall programme for supplying water free of charge to users in the City were running into even more serious difficulties.

Reconstruction work following the Great Fire and new development to the west of the City, in what had formerly been open countryside, were both giving rise to problems. In many cases development was taking place over the top of the existing lead pipes conveying water from Tyburn to the Conduits.

In April 1673 a report was received[200] of one example "in a place by Picadilly, where the foundations for new buildings are laying, the City's pipes are laid open and now lie altogether uncovered and in one of them a hole is made as big as a man's wrist and now stopped up (by those that made it) with a plug. Next to the street going up to Picadilly new buildings are rearing near the City's pipes and a great stack of chimneys already placed upon them which buildings are Colonel Pantons".

There was also mention of the "multitude of buildings erected over the said pipes". A deputation of City worthies, with the Chamberlain, was nominated[201] to "discourse and treat with Colonel Panton touching proposals now represented for better Serving the City's pipes now lying bare and uncovered in several places" and to "consider the removing and new laying of the said pipes". The fact that the deputation was required to "treat" with Col Panton makes it all too clear that the City authorities lacked effective powers of control.

In the same month of April 1673 the Tankard Bearers at Aldgate Conduit petitioned[202] for a supply of water there. This Conduit had fortunately been unaffected by the Great Fire, being located just to the east of the devastated area. The supply was also independent, coming south from springs at Dalston. But here, too, problems had arisen because of development over the pipes and the inevitable irregularly-made connections. In July 1676 it was stated[203] that:

> "... the Citie's Water which used to supply the Conduit at Aldgate is Clandestinely taken away by severall persons Inhabiting the ground under which the Pipes for Conveying the said Water do lye. By meanes whereof the said Conduit is for the present altogether unsupplied with water ..."

The City Plumber and the Comptroller of the Chamber were told:

> "... to endeavour to find out any of the persons who have so injuriously taken away the said Water and make speedy Report thereof unto this Court to the end this Court may direct some effectual prosecution against them".

Exploring housing developments in an effort to discover illegal connections cannot have been easy when the areas were now teeming with people. In one case a surviving receipt[204] shows that the City Chamberlain employed some sort of private sleuth, by name Francis Morris, to whom 20 shillings was paid:

> "on account of satisfaction for my care & paines in discovering some persons who stole the water from the Citie pipes about St James's feilds".

It was not only houses that were being built over the top of the City's aqueducts. About the same time the Court of Aldermen received a letter[205] from the "Earl of St Albans, Lord Chamberlain of his Majesty's Household":

> "... *declareing that a new Church is suddenly intended to be built in St James Markett over part of the Cities pipes, and therefore desireing that this Court would take some speedy care for removeall or security thereof ...*"

With development outside the City proceeding apace, these problems steadily worsened. Shortages of water continued to be caused and became a major cause of concern. Thus in 1685 the City Plumber[206] was instructed to recover the water for the relief of the poor Water-bearers to Cornhill, Gracechurch Street, Honey Lane and Cripplegate Conduits.

The Aldgate Conduit re-supplied

Eventually, the only measure likely to prove effective – realignment of the supply pipelines so that they lay under streets – was undertaken in respect of the Aldgate Conduit, which seems to have been still "unsupplied with water". The general idea of realignment had been considered five years after the Great Fire[207] when the Court of Common Council was asked to consider:

> "... *of removing & carrying ye pipes which convey ye conduit waters into ye Citty into ye heighwayes by reason of ye multitude of building erected upon ye said pipes by reason whereof ye said waters are stollen in greate quantities and ye repaires of ye same pipes being exceeding difficult & chargeable ...*"

But nothing was done at that time and the first positive recommendation came in June 1687 when a report was received stating[208]:

> "... *that to bring the water again to Aldgate Conduit it will be convenient to remove the pipes from under the houses, and lay the same in the street for about the length of two hundred yards and that the charge thereof will probably amount to near £70*"

Instructions were given immediately for this work to be carried out "with the least charge that the same may be done for to the Chamber".

By the time the work was actually carried out in the following year both the extent and the cost had grown considerably. The Contractor's bill for digging the trench[209] (*See* Appendix G) shows that a total length of 750 yards was excavated at a total cost of £141-15s-11d. This was clearly not a cheap solution to the problem, but it seems that this realignment must have been effective in restoring the supply of water to the Aldgate Conduit. For several years no further complaint from either the Water-bearers or the inhabitants of that area is on record.

Difficulties with the principal aqueduct from Tyburn

Four years later the City embarked on a similar, but much more ambitious, project to realign the principal aqueduct feeding water into the City from the west.

In 1692 one Robert Aldersey – described as a "Citizen and Wax-chandler" – was invited[210] by the Corporation to compute the cost of laying new pipes from Tyburn to the City. In September of that year he submitted a proposal[211] whereby the several existing lead pipes from Tyburn to Stocks Market (at the junction of Cornhill and Bread Street) would be taken up and replaced by a single new 5 inch diameter lead main about 3½ miles long which would follow the line of the public streets. Aldersey offered to carry out the whole of this work for £1,000, provided that he was allowed to reclaim and keep all the old lead pipes. As the cost of realigning 750 yards of the Aldgate pipeline earlier had been more than £140 for the trench alone, this must have seemed a reasonable proposition and the City authorities accepted Aldersey's offer[212] in April 1693.

There would clearly be a major threat to the Water-bearers' business if the flow of water to the Conduits were to be interrupted during Aldersey's work on this principal supply line from the west. A month after his contract had been approved[213] the Court of Aldermen received a:

> *"... humble Petition of the Tankard-bearers ... for a Supply of Water from the maine Pipes of the new River water until the Conduit Pipes shall be new laid ..."*

As a result a Committee was instructed to:

> *"... Treat and agree with the Corporation of the new River water for a sufficient supply of Water for the Petitioners Releife for the present ..."*

The result of this approach to the New River Company must presumably have been successful, but details are unknown – the early records of that Company having been destroyed[214] in a fire in 1769.

It may have seemed that the interests of the Water-bearers' business had been safeguarded and that the supply would improve once Aldersey had completed his construction of the new pipeline along its better alignment. But adverse factors now intervened.

Since the Great Fire the City's financial position had become more and more difficult, and active steps were now being taken to generate income from various sources, including its aqueducts. Under the Act of 1680 (Appendix B line 162) the Corporation was empowered to lease out the water in these aqueducts which was surplus to that required for the Conduits, Prisons, etc. The first such lease related to supplies from St Pancras, Hampstead and Hornsey. These were let in December 1692 for a fine of £200 and an annual rent of £80 to a group of individuals headed by financier William Patterson. The same group also secured a lease on the City's waters in Southwark in 1694 for £400 fine and an annual rent of £125.

In February 1694 a Committee "Ordered that the lessees of the Waters do provide according to their Covenants that the Tankard Bearers doe not want imploy for defect of their comeing in And the Lessees being present did promise the same should be done accordingly".

At the same time as Aldersey was laying the new main pipeline to the City the "Committee of Improvements of the Cittyes Revenue" was negotiating with several applicants[215] wishing to take a lease on all the waters tapped off the aqueducts from Marylebone and Paddington. Rapid development west of the City evidently made this appear to be a much more lucrative prospect and the lease was eventually secured by one Thomas Houghton, who agreed to

Conduit head at Paddington.

make an initial payment of no less than £2,650. Annual rent was to be abated to a peppercorn for two years, but thereafter he was to pay a rent of £700 per annum for a further 49 years. Houghton[216] duly made the initial payment on Lady Day 1694, but thereafter the whole arrangement ran into serious difficulties leading to a succession of legal cases which eventually finished up, years later, in the House of Lords.

The problem which arose was initially not financial, but physical. It related to the quantity of water actually delivered by the 5 inch main that Aldersey had laid from Tyburn to the City. In putting forward his initial proposal[217] in 1692 he had stated that:

> *"... According to the best Jugement I could make after soe wett a season as this summer the springs of Paddington and Marylebone collected at the Banquetting House on Tybourne Roade doe afford about Twenty Tuns an hour ..."*

This estimate of water available had presumably been based on measurements at Tyburn, but it had then been assumed that a 5 inch diameter pipe would convey that same amount – 20 tons an hour – to the City. And this same figure had been made known to Houghton during the negotiations for his lease. He had accepted the City's requirement[218] that he was to continue to provide at least 5 tons an hour for the free supplies at the main Conduits, four prisons and a small number of official buildings including the Guildhall and the Session House. But in assessing the potential value of his lease, he had (not unnaturally) assumed that this would leave him with about 15 tons an hour to sell through quills.

In February 1695 the Lord Mayor informed the Court of Common Council[219] that a difference had arisen

> *"... between the Citty and Mr Robert Aldersey for yt he hath not brought into ye Citty as far as the Stocks Markett Nineteen Tons of Water each & every hour according to his Covenant ..."*

Accurate assessment of the quantity of water actually supplied through the new 5 inch main was clearly needed. The Improvements Committee called in both Aldersey and Houghton and it was agreed that "an Experiment be made whether the pipes by now laid by Mr Aldersea will carry 19 Tuns of water an hour pursuant to his agreement". The Court of Aldermen mobilised a remarkable galaxy of talent to carry out the measurements. On 23rd April 1695 Sir Christopher Wren appeared before them[220] and was:

"... desired that hee together with Mr Halley would take the Admeasurement of the Conduit Waters at the Conduit head ... was pleased to promise that the Same should be Effectually performed".

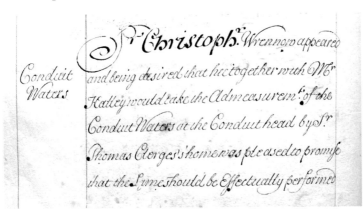

Sir Christopher Wren agrees to admeasure the Conduit flow together with Mr Halley.

A few weeks later Mr Halley (Edmond Halley of "Halley's Comet", no less) submitted a short report[221] showing the differences in level that he had measured between the basin near Tyburn and the Conduit in Cheapside related to High Water mark at Hungerford Stairs. No details of the measurements of flow carried out at that time appear to survive, but Dr Hooke (Robert Hooke of "Hooke's Law", no less) was also called in and from submissions in the later legal proceedings it is clear that the measurements indeed showed the actual quantity delivered by the new pipe to be only 5 or 6 tons per hour.

(At that time, knowledge of hydraulics was rudimentary. Even such luminaries as Halley and Hooke would not have been able to predict by calculation the likely throughput under a given head of a 5 inch pipe 3½ miles long. Present-day calculations show that there was never the slightest prospect of the new pipe delivering 20 tons an hour. For such a throughput, a vastly greater head would have been required than that naturally available from Tyburn to the City).

The original Covenants with Mr Aldersey had included provision for arbitration in the event of any "difference" arising. Two attempts at arbitration[222] were made in 1696, but both failed and it seems that the City's case against Mr Aldersey ultimately finished up in the Court of Chancery.

The repercussions of the dispute widened over the years. Payments of the £700 annual rent ceased and in July 1700 two petitioners who had invested money in Houghton's lease sought[223] to have the rent abated because:

"... the pipe laid by the said Aldersey ... does not bring thither ... above six Tons hourly as has appeared by severall tryalls and

admeasurements by Dr Hooke one of the Citie's Surveyors and Mr Edmond Hally, and other very skillfull and capable Judges in matters of that kind, ..."

Because of the major shortfall in the quantity of water delivered they had "expended considerable sums of money without the least return of profitt or any present expectancey of it". But their appeals proved fruitless, neither the lower Courts nor the House of Lords[224] providing them with any relief. By now Thomas Houghton had become insolvent and one of the petitioners had died and the City had to recover piecemeal[225] parts of the overdue monies.

How Aldersey emerged from this sorry mess is not clear. When summoned in October 1700 to attend a meeting of a Committee re Conduit Waters he declined[226] to answer them on the grounds that he had already "given his answer in Chancery". One forms the impression that he was not seriously inconvenienced. He was a member of Court of the Wax Chandlers Company for many years[227] and was Master of that Company in both 1692–1694 and 1708–1710.

At all events, the City authorities had much less surplus water available for sale than had been expected and their attempt to generate substantial income from this source[228] had proved troublesome. More than 80 years later, in 1782, when the Committee for Letting the City's Lands again sought to lease out the waters from Marylebone and Paddington, the best offer they received[229] was £50 per annum for 7 years – only a small fraction of the £700 per annum they had negotiated with Houghton in 1694. By then the aqueducts were observed to be "in a declining state".

The City loses interest

Throughout the 18th Century the commercial water companies extended both their influence and their areas of supply. Although no definitive pronouncement of policy has been discovered, the overall impression is that after the disappointments and legal battles of the 1690's and early 1700's the City Corporation gradually lost interest in the idea of continuing to make a general supply of water available free of charge. Their attempt to generate a substantial income from their own aqueducts had caused a great deal of trouble and they seem gradually to have accepted that the way ahead lay instead with the various water companies offering water for sale

Indexes[230] to the Repertories – the Minutes of the Court of Aldermen – are suggestive of this change. During many years previously the indexes had recorded dozens of discussions every year under the general heading of "Water", but from about 1700 onwards the number of such entries diminishes sharply and there are no entries at all during 58 years after 1742

The Fraternity declines and disappears

The disastrous effects of the Great Fire in 1666, and all the subsequent difficulties over water supply which are outlined above, must have hit hard the Fraternity of the Water-bearers. They can never again have regained anything like the numbers they had enjoyed in the middle of the 17th Century. The City's cash accounts show that moieties for fines were paid only intermittently after 1666 and the last record of a new member being admitted appears to have been[231] in 1674. The City's own Act of 1680 made no reference to any requirement for payments by the Water-bearers in respect of either admissions or fines, and the last entry[232] in the Cash Accounts under this heading was an isolated payment of 2s 6d in 1684.

Although the number of Water-bearers was much reduced they still continued to have a Fraternity with "Rulers" for at least 65 years after the Great Fire. The evidence for this comes from the lease granted to the Fraternity by the City in 1648 in respect of space for the overhead room at Aldgate Conduit Yard. In June 1731 the Court of Common Council received a report[233] from the Committee for Letting the City's Lands proposing redevelopment in Aldgate Without which referred to:

> *"premises in the possession of the Rulers of the Waterbearers ... granted them at four shillings p.a. and during pleasure".*

Payment of 4s to the City
The City's Cash Accounts[234] confirm that this sum of 4 shillings per annum had *by the Rulers* been paid regularly for more than 80 years. Payments eventually ceased[235] in *of the* 1733, when the accounts showed the item as being "left out by order". *Waterbearers* Although the sum involved was quite small, its regular payment every year *in 1732* shows that the Fraternity must have continued to exist at least up to 1732. *for room at* Thereafter, no evidence has been found showing how much longer the *Aldgate* Fraternity may have remained in being. *Conduit Yard.*

Although the Great Fire suddenly and seriously affected both the business of individual Water-bearers and the fortunes of their Fraternity, it was not the only factor causing their decline. The years following the fire saw other huge, and largely unwelcome, changes for many of the City's Livery Companies[236] brought on by rapid growth of population; expansion of London into areas outside the jurisdiction of the City; and the beginnings of the Industrial Revolution.

The Industrial Revolution was characterised by the replacement of labour-intensive, small-scale working by high-volume production utilising new materials and new technology. Although it took many years, the total replacement of Water-bearers by efficient piped distribution systems was a largely unrecognised element of that revolution. The pioneer castings of iron pipes in France for the water supply to Versailles[237] during the second half of the 17th Century did not achieve the same immediate impact as Abraham Darby's iron bridge over the River Severn at Coalbrookdale in 1779, but in the long run they were just as significant for the progress of mankind.

Disappearance of the Water-bearers' trade

Individual Water-bearers continued to operate for many years after the period when their Fraternity seems to have expired.

During the following years, as traffic in the City continued to grow, each of the Conduits surviving in the streets was demolished so as to remove the obstruction[238]. The last to go appears to have been Lamb's Conduit[239] in about 1755. But the City Corporation retained its rights[240] over the Tyburn Springs until 1812, and the removal of the Conduits by no means marked the final disappearance of the Water-bearers' trade. Even as late as 1851 one author[241] wrote that:

> *"It may be a surprise to many that there are still water carriers in London, and some of them depending on their trade for a livelihood"*

In some cases the reason for this was probably sentimental, as suggested by another writer earlier in that Century[242]:

> *"... the prejudices of old-fashioned people in favour of water brought to the door ... I"ll stick to the carrier as long as he has a pail full and I have a penny ..."*

A Fatal Footnote

The earliest record of a Water-bearer quoted in Chapter 1 was a fatality in 1276 and this history can fittingly conclude with another fatality, 578 years later. This much later fatality was, by chance, documented in detail at the time and although the water involved had originated in the neighbouring City of Westminster, rather than in the City of London, it serves as an example of the persistence of manual distribution arrangements into the 19th Century. It also illustrates how water was, in some cases, carried over remarkable distances – in this case more than 3 miles.

During the first quarter of the 19th Century a family firm of silversmiths by the name of Eley – comprising father and three sons – was well-established in London[243]. After the death of the father in 1824 the three sons branched out into a different line of business, making cartridges and percussion caps: the name of Eley is still associated with that specialised field today. They continued to do well and in March 1841 the eldest brother, William[244], was living in Chelsea with his wife and family – evidently in some comfort, with two servants resident in the house. Later that year he accidentally killed himself in bizarre circumstances[245].

From reports in "The Times"[246] and the Coroner's inquest[247] it emerged that William Eley was in the habit of obtaining from a chemist for his own purposes quantities of fulminate of mercury, the sensitive compound used in percussion caps. When purchased the compound was in wet condition, which rendered it safe to handle, but he then dried it on a metal plate over a boiling kettle in order to weigh it. On 25th June 1841 he was carrying out this procedure on a 2lb consignment of the chemical in rented premises at Emmett's Mews, Bond Street when something must have gone wrong and the fulminate detonated, blowing both William and the room to smithereens. The residents of Old Bond Street and neighbourhood were said to have been thrown into the utmost alarm:

> "... in consequence of a tremendous explosion similar to the discharge of cannon ...".

Despite this setback, the firm of Eley Brothers continued to flourish and by the summer of 1854 had established a percussion cap factory employing about 200 people in Soho at 37, Broad Street. In the meantime Susannah Eley, the widow of William, had moved to West End, Hampstead. She evidently kept in touch with the family firm and every day a large bottle of water from a pump in Broad Street was taken by cart to Hampstead "because she preferred it".

On 31st August 1854 a bottle of this water was taken by carrier, as usual, to Hampstead and Susannah drank some of it that evening. She also drank some more on the following day, but was then taken violently ill and died on

2nd September – the cause of her death being recorded[248] bleakly as *"diarrhoea 2 hours, cholera epidemica 16 hours"*.

Susannah Eley thus became one of the first victims of a virulent cholera epidemic which claimed 126 other victims from Soho that day. Within a week, more than 500 people from that small area had died of the disease, including 18 workers at the percussion cap factory. Most of the surviving residents fled the area.

Susannah's misfortune was recorded in detail by Dr John Snow in his classic treatise[249] on "The Mode of Transmission of Cholera" written shortly after these events. After interviewing many of the survivors and plotting a map of the area showing where those dying of cholera had lived or worked he pointed the finger of blame unerringly at the water pump in Broad Street. The death of Susannah three miles away in Hampstead, where no other cholera was reported at that time was, in Snow's words, "perhaps the most conclusive of all in proving the connexion between the Broad Street Pump and the outbreak of cholera".

The science of water examination and treatment was only just starting to emerge in the mid-Nineteenth Century and Dr Snow had no means of identifying the specific bacterial cause of cholera. But his penetrating epidemiological analyses in various parts of London eventually helped to set in motion the sweeping improvements in water supply (including effective pressurised piped distribution systems) and sanitation which brought enormous benefits to public health in the second half of the Nineteenth Century.

The sad tale of Susannah Eley's death in 1854 forms an appropriate conclusion to this account of the manual distribution of water in London over a period of almost six centuries. From the mid 19th Century onwards both the quality and the quantity of water available began to improve. Her story also provides a link between the past and the present. As the trade of the Water-bearers declined, several instances were recorded of poor people continuing to employ them partly out of sympathy and partly because they did not demand – as the water companies did – a substantial initial outlay of cash. Susannah was quite different. She was well-off (having a servant resident with her in Hampstead) and was willing to pay extra for a particular type of water merely because "she preferred it". In one sense she was therefore a very early forerunner of the many millions of us today who are sufficiently well-off to purchase bottled water because we prefer it.

But we have the advantage that high quality potable water is also available in quantity and under pressure throughout our homes – brought to us by the highly efficient and economical pipe systems which have revolutionised water supply and eliminated the need for manual distribution.

Chapter 5
THE WATER-BEARERS IN RETROSPECT

It may be as well to close this history of the Water-bearers with a brief overview of what has been learnt about them and their Fraternity.

For many hundreds of years the Water-bearers individually provided a very useful service in the City. With the Corporation ensuring (at least for most of the time) a free supply of water at the several Conduits, distribution necessarily had to be carried out manually because of the lack of any piped distribution network such as exists today. A small number of the inhabitants, a few dozen at most, were influential enough to negotiate a "quill" direct off one of the City's aqueducts and some had wells. But there were many thousands of households in which the inhabitants had either to fetch water for themselves, send a servant, or pay a Water-bearer to do the job.

Over the years there must have been a gradual change in the clientele of the Water-bearers. In earliest times only reasonably affluent households will have had enough cash to pay either a servant or a Water-bearer. The arrival of Peter Morice's pumping device in 1582, the New River in 1613 and various other water companies as the years passed, provided the more affluent customers with alternative sources of supply. Increasingly, the customers of the continuing Water-bearers must have been those in the less affluent households who could not afford the capital outlay of a Water Company's connection charge or half-yearly bills.

But the essential features of the Water-bearer's trade changed hardly at all through the Centuries. The men and women waiting their turn at the Conduits and then trudging through the streets bearing a tankard on their shoulders must have been a common sight in the City, which continued essentially unchanged throughout a very long period of London's history. This narrative about their trade has, in places, flitted from Century to Century without any hint of the changing scene around them. A few reminders will illustrate the point.

The start, in 1276, was in Medieval times when many of the City's inhabitants like "John le Tanckardmaker" and "Robert de St Botolph" still retained partly Normanised names. Forty years later, in 1316, torrential rain ruined much of the harvest in England and about one in twelve of the population starved to death[250]. In 1357 a City proclamation[251] announced a ban on the export of bows or arrows. In 1496, when the Water-bearers Fraternity gained their Ordinances, Columbus[252] had discovered Jamaica, but not yet the mainland of America. The population of the City of London in 1276 was probably less than 100,000. By the end of this narrative, the population of Greater London had grown to more than 2½ million and the Industrial Revolution was well under way.

At various times during this long period the City was beset by disturbances great and small. These included Wat Tyler's insurrection[253] in 1381, when a mob beheaded many unpopular citizens in Cheapside, the Vintry and elsewhere; and the food riots and those of apprentices[254] in 1595. The Water-bearers' trade was essential from day to day, and most of them presumably had to carry on as best they could while these commotions went on around them in the streets.

So far as the Fraternity is concerned, the account in Chapter 2 concluded with the period from 1562 to 1666 during which the organisation flourished, attaining a membership probably in excess of 500. Prior to that period, and particularly before the Reformation in 1534, the Fraternity had a significant association with an important religious house – Austin Friars – and was doubtless much less under the control of the City authorities. Surviving records of that earlier period are scarce, but the fact that an organisation started by fewer than 40 members in 1496 had secured its own "Hall" by 1568 suggests that it had not been unsuccessful in securing both members and some degree of status in the community.

Members of the Fraternity were manual workers at the bottom end of the social scale, the great majority doubtless illiterate, and the earnings of most of them must have been pitifully small by present-day standards. Yet their organisation vigorously defended the interests of its members, submitting many petitions to the City authorities and even, on one occasion, to Parliament.

It is difficult to tell, after this lapse of time, how much influence the Fraternity's repeated representations may have had on the City authorities or the Government. But their petitions were sometimes backed up by residents of areas served by particular Conduits and when they complained of shortages of water they must have had the general support not only of their own customers but also of everyone else who made use of that particular Conduit.

In the long term, the Fraternity's petitioning must have been one of the factors leading to the City's repeated extensions of the aqueduct system. And in the short term they certainly had occasional successes in particular areas. For instance, during the City's disagreement with the College of Physicians over its "quill" in 1618 the Minutes of the Court of Aldermen[255] recorded that:

> *"... the said doctors have promised they would ymploye one or more of the said clamorous Water bearers during the scarcity of water taking them water for the service of their house".*

The overall impression is that during much of its life the Fraternity was an effective and useful organisation which served well both the inhabitants of the City and its own members. That it eventually ceased to exist need not be a cause for surprise. Unwin[256] points out that of 111 craft organisations known to have been in existence in 1473, a considerable number "disappeared or were absorbed by their more successful rivals". The manual distribution of water was not the only trade that was eventually superseded – other crafts unknown today in the list of 1473 included the Galochemakers, the Writers of Court Letters and the Orglemakers.

List of figures

Acknowledgements

A cautious approach to history

History can be perilous stuff. Depending, as it does, on contemporary accounts which themselves may be true, biased, mistaken or even plain lies, it then has superimposed on these uncertainties the mistakes, personal approach, and perhaps prejudices, of the individual historian. Anyone reading the two books about the First World War by Alan Clarke[257] and John Terraine[258] must marvel that two authors can come up with totally different interpretations of events which took place not so very long ago. Readers have to make up their own minds as to which of these two accounts they think is correct – or perhaps it is neither?

In the limited field of this history of the Water-bearers we have come across several statements about their Fraternity of the Brotherhood of St Christopher which we question. The most significant is Overall's statement[259] in a book published in 1871 that "this company appears by an entry in ... Letter Book B to have existed as early as 1276". Careful examination of the relevant entry in Letter Book B shows that Overall's suggestion was groundless. He apparently jumped to the conclusion that, because there was a recognised occupation of "Water-carrier", there must also have been some sort of fraternity. His statement has been repeated in more definite terms by many later authors, including Harben in his popular "Dictionary of London"[260]. We have found no evidence whatever of the existence of a Brotherhood at that very early date. And in the general context of the development of other Fraternities and Companies in the City of London, many of them relating to much more affluent specialities and trades, it seems exceedingly unlikely. Later, one over-enthusiastic author[261] even referred to the "Honourable Company of Water Tankard bearers" – a title which was certainly never authorised.

A further mistake has arisen from the statement that the Fraternity was dissolved by the City[262] in 1553 which, though correct in itself, has led some later authors to assume that it never re-emerged. But surviving records of the

Corporation show conclusively that the Fraternity was re-established a few years later and continued to exist for at least another 180 years – and for much of that time it flourished. The oft-repeated suggestion that the Water-bearers lived mainly in Cobb's Court[263] also appears to be unsubstantiated.

In the list of References which concludes this history we have quoted from a wide range of documents, some of which we regard as more dependable than others. We have relied heavily on primary (contemporary) sources; on transcripts and Calendars of early documents painstakingly prepared by such specialists as Sharpe and Riley; and on a small number of authoritative books, particularly that by Unwin. Elsewhere we have tried to substantiate statements made in printed books, but this has not always been possible, particularly where the authors have not recorded the sources of their statements. The comprehensive lists of references will allow future researchers to check, and we hope verify, our findings and conclusions.

Acknowledgements

A retired civil engineer and a chemical engineer launching out into such dangerous and uncharted waters need a pilot, and we have been fortunate to have the advice and assistance of Laura Wright, the Honorary Archivist of the Water Conservators Company. At an early stage in our studies she persuaded us of the vital importance of keeping a proper record of the References consulted. Over a period of three years this has grown to several stout files of papers including photocopies and transcripts from nearly 300 documents – half of them primary sources.

Apart from ensuring this degree of discipline, Laura also made two other major contributions to our work. First, she has helped us with transcribing several pre-1600 documents which, though written in the English language, are in Secretary Hand, which we initially found very difficult to read. A short example is shown opposite to illustrate the difficulty. Laura's other major contribution was to suggest that we contact Mark Jenner, a lecturer in history at the University of York. That was a fruitful idea. Mark is currently carrying out research on water in Early Modern London and proved to be most helpful. We have followed up several of the references provided in his excellent article in "Londinopolis" published by Manchester University Press in 2000. We have also had discussions with him and he kindly read through and commented on a draft of this text. It has been very useful to have his comments.

Much of our research, particularly into printed books, has been carried out in the Guildhall Library where the staff have been unfailingly helpful and we should like to extend our thanks to them. Our work on primary sources has largely been carried out in the Corporation of London Record Office (CLRO),

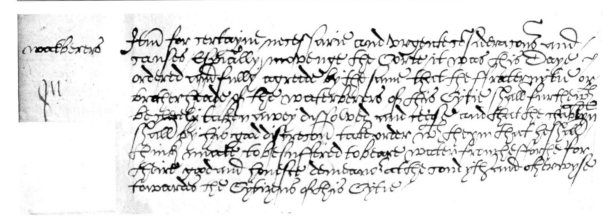

'Item for certayne necessarie and vrgente consderacions and causes Especially movenge the Corte it was this Daye ordered and fully agreede by the same that the ffraternytie or brotherhood of the waterbearers of this Cyte shall futhewith be clerely taken awey dissolved and cease ...' (from Repertory 13 in 1553)

which is also housed in the Guildhall. A gratifying number of the Corporation's original manuscript records have survived flood and fire over many centuries and, as can be seen from the lists of references, these were the source of many of our findings about the Water-bearers. The staff of the CLRO have been most helpful and we must express our gratitude to them for all their many kindnesses.

We have received useful information, quoted in these pages, from the Archivists of the Coopers Company, the Society of Apothecaries of London and the Wax Chandlers Company, and from the Librarian of the Goldsmiths Company – to all of whom we extend our thanks. We have also been helped by many other individuals including Stanley Heather, Michael Rouse, Bill Harding, Geoff Saul, John Clark at the Museum of London, Maarten Prak, Michael Thorn, Ian Staniforth, Gwilym Roberts and Peter Martin as well as staff at Thames Water, London Metropolitan Archives, the British Museum, the University of London Library, Edinburgh University Library, the Bodleian Library, the Bodleian Law Library, the House of Lords Record Office and the British Library. To all of them our thanks are due.

The design of this volume has been carried out for us in two stages, first by Rachel Howe and secondly by Martin Cox, both of whom have made useful suggestions and accommodated our detailed requirements with skill and accuracy. Colin Bland commented usefully on an early draft and kindly "scanned" many of the pictures for us.

In conclusion, we should perhaps point out that this book cannot pretend to be a final and definitive history of the Water-bearers. Although we have attempted to consult original records where they are in English, neither of us has any useful knowledge of Latin which is the language of the earliest records. We have concentrated much of our attention at CLRO on the "Repertories", ie the Minutes of the Court of Aldermen, and the City's Cash records but there is a multitude of other sources which we have not attempted to consult in depth.

Some of the Calendars published by dedicated individuals like Riley and Sharpe a century or so ago have been most useful, but we have generally relied on their indexes to find relevant pieces of information. This is a procedure which saves a lot of time, but inevitably may result in some items being missed. Indexing these older publications by manual methods must have been a laborious procedure, which was clearly less-than-perfect in many cases. But we hope that this account may prove useful to any future researcher in this field.

The responsibility for any errors is, of course, ours.

Appendices

APPENDIX A

The Ordinances of 1496

*Note: With one exception, we have reproduced here the Water-bearers'
Ordinances of 1496 exactly as they appeared in Coote's paper to the London
and Middlesex Archaeological Society which was published in January 1871 in
their Proceedings Vol IV Part 1 on pages 55-58. This was soon after their
discovery, along with the Ordinances of five other secular Guilds, by Tyssen in
the records of the Commissary Court of London. The one exception is that we
have added paragraph numbers in order to facilitate references in Chapter 2
to sections of the Ordinances.*

RULES, ORDENAUNCES, AND STATUTES made by the RULERS, WARDENS,
and the hoole FELISHIP of the Brotherhed of SAINT CHRISTOFER of the
WATERBERERS of the CITIE of LONDON, founded and ordeyned in the FRERE
AUGUSTINYS of LONDON and acknowledged before THOMAS BRENT Doctor
of Law and Commissary of London; the See then being void. 20 October 1496, 12
Henry VII

Theese been the Statutes that beth made by the wardens and the hoole Fellship of the
Brotherhed of Saint Christofer of the Waterberers founded withyn the Friers
Augustines in London as folowith.

1. First hit is ordeyned that ther shall no man chese the wardens of the seid Fraternitye
but onely they that have been wardyns and they that bith for the yere.

2. Also hit is ordeyned that there shall no brother nor sister arrest none of hys seid
brothers nor sisters without licence of the wardens that be and the wardens that have
been byfore tyme undre the payne of vjs viij d to the boxe

3. Also hit is ordeyned that if ther be eny man or woman of the seid Brotherhed that
wil not obbey the statutes that been made in this behalf but frowardly wille disobbey

them he for to pay iij s. iiij d.

4. Also it is ordeyned that if ther be any man or woman of the said feliship that revileth ony of them that beth wardens or have been wardens of the same Feliship and callith them otherwise than they owght to doo be it brother or sister then if it be a man that so doth he for to pay 111j li wex and if it be a woman she for to pay ij li wex as oftentymes as it may be provid eny of them so offendith this statute.

5. Also it is ordeyned that if ther be eny brother or sister of the seid Brotherhed that dieth withyn the franches of the said Citiee of London than that persone that so deceaseth shal have the torches and the tapers of the said Fraternite if so be that they do ther dieuty to the seid Brotherhed as they shold doo.

6. Also it is ordeyned that they that beth wardens of the Feliship for the yere shall do no correccion without they do first take counsell of them that hath been wardeyns afore tyme that thann the seid wardens that have been before tyme shall stond by them in all that is rightfulle and lawfull and they forto ber with them their mony like as they doo and if the seid wardens for the tyme being wille not doo as is aforesaid eche of them for the yere beyng shall paye v li of wex as often as they so offendith.

7. Also it is ordeyned that if the seid wardens that have been byfore tyme wilnot stande by them that beth wardens for the yere in all ryght when they calle them then they for to pay a peece vj li. wex as often as the wardens for the yere being calle them.

8. Also it is ordeyned that if there be eny brother of (sic) sister of the Fraternite aforesaid that removeth out of the seid Cite of London that he shalbe don for if he decease and have doon his diuety than he shal have his Masse and his Dirige with the torches and tapers as a brother shuld have or a sister that deceaseth in the foresaid Cite of London.

9. Also if ther be any man or woman of the seid Fraternite warned to come to the byrying of eny brother or sister that dieth withyn the Cite of London and come not if that he have no lawfull excuse he or she so faylyng for to pay j li. of wax as often as he or she is warned and so fayleth.

10. Also if ther be eny brother or syster that takeyth eny custemar owt of eny brothers handys without so be that the parties that he serveth wille no lengar have his service and that the seid brother seith that he be content of his diewte that he shold have or ellis he to take no mannys custymer owt of hys hands under the payne of vj s. viij d. be hit brother or syster.

11. Also it is ordeyned that if there be eny brother or syster that heryth any of our counsell withyn our selfe and uttereth it and will not kepe it wythyn our selfe that they shall pay 111j li. wex as often tymes as it may be knowen and lawfully proved so that the seid counsell be not contrary to the lawes of the Chirch nor prejudiciall to the Kyng and this realme of England.

12. Also it is ordeyned that if eny brother or syster of the seid Fraternite take into ther service eny persone not beying a brother of the same Fraternite that then the seid persone shalbe presentid byfore the wardens for the tyme beyng withyn iij dayes after he shall so be set a werk. And to paye at hys presentment j li. of wex to the use of the seid Fraternite. And this to be doon uppon the payne of forfayture of ij li. wax. And costys and charges of every such brother so doyng to the contrary to be convertid to the seid use.

13. Providid alwey that if any of the seid transgressouris beyng a brother or a sister of the seid fraternite fortune to be of such poverte and insufficientnesse that he or she is not able to pay the seid hole ffynes and forfeitures or ellis if eny other consideracion or remorce of consciens or pite canne be thought in suche losses or forfeitures that conscience or pite wolde not that they shulde not be hole levied that then by the advise of the undrewriten Ordinary Juge or his successors and of the seid rulers and governors of the seid fraternite for the tyme beyng the seid fynes and forfaitures by grace shalbe mitigat and lessid as the case shall require after ther discrecions.

14. In the name of God Amen. We Thomas Brent Doctor of Law and Commissary of London the see ther being voied to all Christen people to whome this present writing shal come or shall hereof know send gretyng in our Lord God. And where it is so that of late the rulers and wardens of the Brotherhed of Seint Christofere foundyd and ordeyned by Waterberers of the Cite of London in the Frere Augustinys of London aforeseid and the Brethern of the seid Fraternite that is to sey William Johnson, John Kerver and John Parker now beinge rulers and wardens of the seid Fraterniite, John Gregori, Thomas Johnson, John Raynoldson, Robert Savage, Robert Digonson, John Baker, Richard Payn, John Bager, John Lesby, Thomas Mores, John Smere, John Cakes, Elis Brian, Thomas Lambe, Jeffrey Blake, William Smyth, David Breupine, Jacobe Offzand, Simond Wryght, Richard Payne, John Maston, Richard Trowyll, Harry Barbour, William Aylmer, William Cornyshe, Robert Long, John Goodfeld, John Browne, Thomas Payne, John Bland, John Watson, John Byckyrs, Thomas Somer, Thomas Nepecker, and Nicholas Thomson being alle or the more parte or greter parte of the Fraternite aforeseid have with good mynde and to thentent of good rule to be hadde and kepte in the seid Fraternite in tyme comynge with gret instances had in this party presentid unto us all suche rules ordinaunces and statutes as bith above wryten with one statut folowing in the end mekely besechyng and desyring us the Commissary aforeseid to ratify, stablilish, auetorise and conferme the seid rules, ordinaunces and statutes:

15. We therefore Thomas Brent Doctor and Commissary aforeseid consideryng that the seid beseeching and desire been resonable and consonant to good law and consciens with the consent of the seid rulers, wardens and brethren ratify, stabilishe, auetorysze and conferme as fer as in us all and singler rules and ordinaunces and statutes above specified especially charging the said rulers, wardens and brethern all and eche of them that they and eche of them doo duly and truly obbey, observe, and kepe all the seyd rules, ordinaunces and statutes as it to them and ether of them concernith and to them perteynithe undre payne of the grete curse and other paynes

expressed in the same statutes, ordinaunces and rules and for the more feith and credence to be geven to this present writinge we the seid Commissary have putt to this writinge, rules, ordinaunces and statutes our seale of office the xx day of Octobre the yere of our Lord God Mccclxxxxvj and in the xij yere of the reigne of Kyng Henry the vijth.

16. Also hit is ordeyned that no brother or syster of the seid Fraternyte shal have at the condyte at onys to his owne use above one tankard uppon the payne of li. of wex to the use of the lyght aforeseid to be applyed.

Wm. Fox, Registrar

APPENDIX B

The City's Act of 1680

Note: The following is a transcript of Journal 49 fos 140 – 142b, being the Minutes of the Court of Common Council on 7th October 1680. The major part of the entry is the Act concerning Aqueducts, but this is followed (from line 245) by an item dealing with the financing of the "extraordinarily ornamental" Conduit at the upper end of Cheapside with its 160 ft high obelisk and other incidental works.

Line numbers have been added in order to facilitate detailed referencing in the text.

Fo 140
Report Aqueducts

At This Court the Committee appointed to consider of the
Bill concerning the AqueDucts and Conduitts of this Citty brought
in A Report touching the same together with the said Bill, the
5 form of which Report followeth in these words vizt

The Right honourable the Lord Major Aldermen
and Commons of the Citty of London in Common
Councell assembled

Wee whose names are subscribed in pursuance of an order of
0 this Honourable Court date the 17th of March 1679 Referring to us the
perusall and further consideracion of a Bill concerning the AqueDucts
and Conduits of this Citty severall times Read in and Considered Here by
this Court have severall times met perused and considered of the said
Bill and with some few alteracions which we here present with the said
5 Bill we are of opinion that it is a very usefull and necessary Bill fit to
be enacted and speedily published and put in execucion the delayes
of the particulars thereof for many yeares having been very prejudiciall
to this Citty All which notwithstanding we submit to the consideracion
of this Honourable Court Dated the sixth day October 1680

0

John DuBois   Robt Clayton Major
John Oliver   E Turgis
         Ralph Box

Ater the reading of which Report and of the said Bill paragraph
by paragraph the said Bill after some few Amendments here made
5 was passed and made the Act of this Court the tenor whereof followeth

Act for the AqueDucts passed

For as much as it is of great importance and absolute necessity
to this Citty and the Inhabitants thereof to have sweet and
wholesome running waters and fresh springs to serve the
30   same for their business and properties And whereas the
Major and Co*mmon*alty and Citizens of this Citty

Fo 140b

have heretofore with great travaile and paines and
to their great Costs and Charges procured and purchased
to themselves a free Liberty to enter into the grounds and
35   possessions as well of the Kings most Excellent Majesty
as of all and every other person and persons and bodies
politique and Corporate, where they shall find or know
any such springs to be, and therein to dig pitts trenches
and Ditches to erect leads, lay pipes, make vaults, and to
40   doe all and every thing and things in the said places
and grounds, most convenient and necessary for the
conveyance of the said waters and springs to the
said Citty and suburbs thereof and are alsoe fully and
absolutely vested with such Authorities and powers as
45   well by several antient and Royall Charters as by
divers Acts of Parliament and more particularly
by a certain Act of Parliament made in the five
and thirtieth yeare of the Reigne of King Henry
the eight as by the same (Relacion being thereunto
50   had) appeareth And by vertue thereof, this Citty hath
been before this time well furnished and abundantly
served with wholesome water and springs But since
the late Dreadfull fire which happened in London the
accustomed Course of waters comeing from the old
55   Springs and antient Heads are diminished aborted or
diverted by private persons contrary to the true intention
of the said Act of Parliament. And that very great
quantityes of the said water hourly run of wast at
the spring heads to the great discommodity and
60   displeasure both of the Cittizens and Inhabitants
within this City and suburbs thereof and of all
other persons having recourse to the same and to
the great decay of ye trade and publick weale of the
same.
65   And forasmuch as this Citty for divers yeares
past hath beene and alsoe must of necessity forthwith
be at very great Charges and Expenses for and toward

the Rebuilding repairing amending and restoring
of the severall Cisterns Conduits and other conveniences
70 both for the receipt and conveyance of the said
waters belonging to this Citty the greatest part
of which within the said Citty were destroyed by the
said Dreadfull Conflagracion and must from time
to time hereafter be also enforced to disburse
75 and expend great sumes of money in and about
the severall heads and pipes of the said springs
and waters in repairing preserving and maintaining
the same for the publick Comodity and Common
good of this Citty Bee it therefore Enacted by the
80 right honourable the Lord Major and Aldermen and Commons
in this Common Counsell assembled and it is hereby
Granted that it shall and may be lawfull to
and for such Committee as this Court shall thinke
fitt from time to constitute and appoint And they
85 are hereby fully impowered forthwith to take
care of and formally provide for as well the

Fo 141

the removing and laying of the severall pipes for conveying of
the said waters as also the making of publick cisterns and
Conduits to receive the same in such convenient places in and
90 about this Citty for the Cittizens and Tankard bearers to resort unto
and fetch water Gratis and to preserve stores of water in Case
of any suddaine and outragious fire as from time to time shall
be found most expedient to the said Committee with the Approbacion
of this Court in as ample manner as by the late Act of
5 Parliament for rebuilding of the City of London the Major
Aldermen and Commonalty by order of Common Councell are Enabled to
doe And be it further enacted by the Authority aforesaid that it
shall and may be lawfull to and for the Committee so as aforesaid
from time to time to be chosen And they are hereby Authorized
10 and impowered to exercise and put in execution all and every
the powers and authorities granted unto and vested in the
Major and Commonalty and Cittizens of the City of London in and
by any antient Royall or other Charter or Charters Grant or
Grants Act or Acts of parliament for and concerning the
15 digging and conveying of any springs and waters to the said
Citty or for and concerning any Conduits pipes Cisterns stores
or receptacles whatsoever for the conveying or preserving the said
springs and waters from time to time and in as full and
ample manner as the said Major and Commonalty and Cittizens
20 at any time before the making of this Act have or might have

Lawfully used enjoyed and exercised the same And the said
Committe are hereby authorized and impowered to make the best
improvement of all Springs and waters belonging or that may
hereafter be discovered to belong to the Major and Commonalty and
115   Cittizens aforesaid over and above such porcions of the said waters
as shall be thought necessary to supply the said publick Conduits
for the purposes aforesaid And to that end to treat and agree
with any person or persons that shall desire to have any of the
said waters conveyed into his or their house or houses And to
120   grant and order to be made a Lease or Leases of the same not
exceeding the terme of Eleaven yeares if the party or parties
to whom such Lease or Leases shall or may be soe made, shall soe
long live and inhabit in such house or houses where the same
water is to be used And be it further enacted by the Authority
125   aforesaid that all Leases granted, or ordered to be made
by the Committee above mencioned in pursuance of this Act
shall be made and subscribed by the Comptroller of the
Chamber for the time being, and the whole Rents thereby
received and the profits thereof to be made shall be made
130   payable into the Chamber of London halfe yearly And the
said Comptroller is hereby authorized to demand receive and
have for the making subscribing and Registering of every
Lease of every Lessee living within the said Citty of London and
Liberties thereof the sum of five shillings and noe more
135   And of every Lessee living without the said Citty and
liberties thereof the sum of ten shillings and noe more
And be it further enacted by the authority aforesaid
the all Leases granted or ordered to be made by the
Committee aforesaid in pursuance of this Act shall be
140   inscribed and Registered by the Chamberlain of the
said City for the time being And sealed with the
Comon seale of the said Citty And that the said

Fo 141b

Chamberlain shall and may demand receive and have
for subscribing and attending the sealing every Lease
145   of each Lessee living within the said Citty of
London and Liberties thereof the sum of one
shilling and eight pence and noe more and of
every Lessee living without the said Citty and
Liberties thereof the sum of three shillings and
150   four pence and noe more And for receiving collecting
and writing a discharge for every halfe yeares rent
of each Lessee living within the said Citty and Liberties
thereof four pence and noe more. And for every Lessee

living without the said Citty and Liberties thereof
55   the sum of eight pence and no more. And be it
further enacted by the authority aforesaid that
it shall and may be lawfull at any time or times
hereafter for the said Committee appointed or to be
appointed by this Court if they shall judge it fitting and
50   advantagious for the benefitt of the Chamber of
London to treat and agree with any person or persons
for a Lease or Leases of the proffitts arising by the
Rents of the said waters over and above what may
from time to time liberally supply the said publick
55   Conduits under such Rent or Rents Covenants Consideracions
and agreements and with such securityes for the payment
and performance thereof, as to them shall seem meet the
monies or rents arising thereby to be paid into the Chamber
of London, And the said Committee to report their proceedings
70   unto this Court for their approbacion therein And thereupon
such person or persons as shall be so agreed withall is are
and shall be hereby authorized and fully impowered with
by and unto all the powers and authorities hereby enacted
for collecting and receiving the said Rents and proffitts of
75   the said waters to his or their owne proper use. And bee
it further Enacted by the authority aforesaid that the
said public Cisterns and Conduits shall be opened every
morning from Ladyday to Michaelmas at five of the
Clock and continue open until eleaven and in the afternoon
0   at one of the Clock and continue open till Eight at night.
And from Michaelmas to Ladyday at seven of the Clock in
the forenoon and continue open till eleaven And at
one of the Clock in the afternoon and continue open
till five or such other hours as hereafter shall be
5   Directed by the authority of this Court And that all
Cittizens and Inhabitants of this Citty by themselves
their servants or Tankardbearers shall have free Liberty
at the said hours to fetch the said waters Gratis
without disturbance And that Especiall Care be
0   taken by the Committee aforesaid fo the time being
for the constant supplyes of the said Conduits and
Cisterns with most plentifull provisions of water
at the hours aforesaid And that no private Quill be
grafted until the Committee aforesaid have appointed
5   the places for the severall publick Cisterns and
Conduits as aforesaid and new layd and settled
the maine pipes leading thereunto so that such
private Quills do not hinder or divert the constant
supply and keeping up of the waters in the said

200   publick Cisterns and Conduits, Any cause matter or thing

fo 142

or things in the Act contained to the contrary notwithstanding
And that all Tankards hereafter to be used at the said publick Cisterns
and Conduits by any Common Tankard Bearers may be of a like measure
Be it Enacted by the authority aforesaid That as well old Tankards
205   already made as all such as shall be hereafter made shall be sealed at
Guildhall by the Hall keeper for the time being as all other Measures are, so
that the same may contain the just and full measure of three
Gallons and a pottle of Winchester Measure at the least And the said
Hall keeper shall receive and take and is hereby authorised to receive
210   and take for the sealing of every such Water tankard the Rate and sume of four
pence and noe more. And that every of the present Tankard Bearers shall
within six months after the publishing of this Act procure a Certificate
from the Alderman or Deputy and Common Counsell men of the respective
Wards wherein they live that they are freemen of the Citty or Widdows of
215   freemen and persons of sober and honest conversation And that all
Tankard Bearers to be allowed shall weare a plate of pewter marked with
the sign of the Conduit whereat they ply and the Citty arms over it the
same to be provided for them by the Hall keeper aforesaid, who is hereby
authorized to receive for every such plate one shilling and no more.
220   And for the preventing and determining all Differences and strifes
that may hereafter arise or happen between such Tankard Bearers as
shall be imployed at the said publick Cisterns and Conduits It is
further enacted by the authority aforesaid That the Chamberlain of
the said Citty for the time being shall (as formerly) heare mediate and
225   determine all such differences and strifes And all and every such
Tankard Bearers are hereby required and enjoyned to yeild due obedience
and conforme themselves to all such Orders and dispositions as shall
from time to time be made and ordained therein And upon complaint
and due prove made to the Lord Major of this City for the time
230   being of any of the said Tankard Bearers not conforming to such
orders and rules as are herein beforemencioned and appointed
such Tankard bearer may by the said Lord Major or Chamberlain be
either suspended or totally discharged as in their discretions shall be
found most reasonable.

235   Committee for the Aqueducts chosen

And in pursuance of the Saide Act This Court doth now
nominate and appoint the Same Committee who brought in the Said
Report vizt the Right Honourable Sir Robert Clayton Knight Lord Major of this Citty
Sir William Turner and Sir Joseph Sheldon Knights Aldermen Sir Thomas Player Knt
240   Mr John Oliver Mr Thomas Vernon Mr Ralph Box Mr John Dubois and Mr

Deputy Turgis Commoners to put in present execucion the said Act according
to the powers and authorities thereby granted them and the true intent
thereof untill another Committee shall be chosen for that purpose by this
Court

45   Cheapside Conduit
     Report

This day the Committee for the Aqueducts to whom the Consideration how
and out of what Cash the charge of erecting A Conduit at the upper
end of Cheapside might be defrayed was referred brought in a Report
50   to this Court touching the same (the tenor whereof followeth vizt)

To the Right Honourable the Lord Major Aldermen and Commons of
the Citty of London in Comon Councell assembled
In persuance of an order of this Common Court bearing date the 17 day
of March 1679 Referring it to us to consider how and out of what Cash
55   the Charge of the Conduit at the upper end of Cheapside lately ordered
to be erected may be borne and defrayed Wee whose names are
subscribed having duly considered thereof do humbly Certifie our
opinions to be that the charge of the said Conduit which is
designed for the publick benefit and advantage of this whole
60   Citty ought to be defrayed by the generall Contribucions thereof
by the way of fifteenths to be appointed and collected by
order of this Honourable Court as in like cases hath beene heretofore antiently and frequently used and accustomed And that for

fo 142b

the more speedy dispatch of so usefull a worke
65   untill the said fifteenths are collected the Committee
with whome this affair shall be entrusted may be impowered
by this Honourable Court to order Mr Chamberlain of London to
disburse by way of Loan out of the sheriffes fines such
sum or sums of money as to them shall seeme necessary
70   for the carrying on thereof to be reimbursed to the said
Cash by the said fifteenths when collected as aforesaid
All which nevertheless wee submit humbly to the great
wisdome of this honourable Court Dated the tenth of August
1680

75
E Turgis   Robt Clayton Major
John DuBois   Tho Player
John Oliver

four fifteenths to be raised

to erect A Conduitt in
280   Cheapside & repairing
Billingsgate Stayer and
others etc

Upon reading whereof and after some debate thereupon
285   it was agreed and ordered by this Court that four fifteenths
each fifteenth to amount to 500l be forthwith raised
upon the severall Inhabitants of this Citty according to
the antient custom and practice as well to defray the
charge of erecting the said Conduit in Cheapside as also
290   A conduit in Aldermanbury and another in Lothbury
And also repairing or making new the former
stayres at Billingsgate Insertion (A) & Pauls Wharfe now

(A) As likewise an house of Easement with
A Room and a belfry over it for the
295   accommodacion of the Markett there
kept, And the repairing or making
new the Stayres at Pauls Wharfe

represented to this Court to be very defective Insertion B And

(B) or any other stayres on this side
300   the Thames, as the said Committee
shall think fitt

This addicion or Amendment in the
Margin was made by order of
Comon Councill on 13th of May
1681   James Gibson
305

this Court doth direct and order that the said moneys
to be raised by the said four fifteens when collected
and received shall be paid into the Chamber of London
and imployed for the works aforesaid And further
that in case any inhabitant or inhabitants in or near
310   any of the said Wards where the said Conduits and
stayres respectively are situate or to be erected shall
and doe Advance any sume or sumes of money to be
laid out and expended in erecting or repairing such
Conduit or stayres before the said fifteenths shall be
315   raised That then such Conduit or stayres for which such
moneys shall be advanced, shall be first gone in hand
with and erected or repaired with the said moneys
and in such case Mr Chamberlain is hereby ordered

20 to pay and reimburse such person or persons so
advancing out of the said moneys to be raised
by the said fifteenths as the same shall come in
alwaies preferring and paying those first that
first advanced such moneys And the rest in order
according to the time of their advancing

25 Fifteenths

And this Court doth refer it to the Committee now
appointed for putting in Execusion the Act for the
Aqueducts and Conduits speedily to advise and consider
of the manner and method of raising the said
30 fifteenths to make an equall and just apportionmnt
thereof upon the severall Wards and to direct and
cause the sume to be raised and paid accordingly

APPENDIX C

Wills of Water-bearers

From Index volumes published by the British Record Society it has been possible to trace and transcribe 26 Wills (or Administrations) of Water-bearers proved in London between 1394 and 1675. These Wills were proved in the Archdeaconry Court of London, the Deanery of the Arches and the Commissary Court of London (London Division). Very much larger numbers of Wills, generally those of the better-off, were also proved at the Prerogative Court of Canterbury, but a search through the indexes[264] covering 1676 to 1700 has not revealed a single Will of a Water-bearer.

Considering the hundreds, if not thousands, of Water-bearers that must have operated in London during these centuries it is clear that the great majority did not leave Wills: this might be expected of people engaged in such a humble trade. Comparison with three other transport Guilds covered by the same Index volumes for London shows that fewer Water-bearers left Wills than any of the other groups. Compared with 26 Water-bearers, there were entries relating to 146 Watermen, 104 Porters and 87 Carmen.

The testators of these 26 Wills were all men, and usually the main, or only, beneficiary was the surviving wife. In many cases the testator did not make any specific bequests, merely referring to his "goods" or "worldly goods". When Thomas Dabbes made his Will in 1618 he referred to "my worldlie goods being but a poore estate".

Six of the testators made specific bequests which can be summarised as follows:

John Jennes in 1543 made two bequests of xiid each

Thomas Harrison in 1590 left a kettle and a quart pewter pot, together with two debts of 9s 4d and 9s respectively

Walter Farmer in 1622 left three bequests of £5 each

Mark Burton in 1615 left two bequests each of a guinea and one of £10

Christopher Garth in 1603 left a substantial assortment of clothing to various relatives and friends including the Minister of his Parish and the Parish Clerk. Items included two morning gowns, a favourite gown, a lined cloak without sleeves, a cloak with sleeves, buff hose and a red fustian doublet, cloth hose and doublet, a black doublet and "working apparel of the better sort". His wife had evidently predeceased him and he left to various female relatives and friends her best gown, her second gown, two black kirtles of stuff and a piece of cloth of gold. Other items listed included brass candle sticks and pewter pots.

William Wilkinson, who was both a Water-bearer and a Girdler, left an altogether different type of Will in 1556 which included an annuity of £30 for his wife out of a farm in Yorkshire.

Each of the Wills states the Parish of the deceased, as shown in the list below, together with the probate date and source reference:

1 Adam, John	1446	St Alban Wood Street	BRS Volume 82 Page 2
2 Bird, Simon	1673	St Giles in the Fields	BRS Volume 102 Page 68
3 Burton, Mark	1615	St Mildred Poultry	BRS Volume 97 Page 70
4 Cholmley, Jn	1569	St Mary Woolnoth	BRS Volume 86 Page 57
5 Dabbes, Tho	1618	St Bride Fleet Street	BRS Volume 97 Page 112
6 Davys, Ellis	1630	All Hallows the Less	BRS Volume 89 Page 104
7 Farmer, Walter	1622	St Ann Blackfriars	BRS Volume 97 Page 143
8 Gaborne, Wm	1608	St Mary Magdalene OFS	BRS Volume 89 Page 153
9 Garth, Chris	1603	St Lawrence Pountney	BRS Volume 97 Page 164
10 Gill, Nich	1543	St Steven Coleman St	BRS Volume 86 Page 109
11 Glover, Tho	1551	St Mary Abchurch	BRS Volume 89 Page 153
12 Gregory, Tho	1632	St Dionis Backchurch	BRS Volume 98 Page 251
13 Harrison, Thos	1590	St Alban Wood Street	BRS Volume 97 Page 196
14 Hullett, Hugh	1675	St Giles in the Fields	BRS Volume 102 Page 363
15 Jacob, Jn	1394	St Michael Cornhill	BRS Volume 82 Page 104
16 Jennes, Jn	1543	St Steven Coleman St	BRS Volume 86 Page 149
17 Kees, Tho	1556	St Clement Eastcheap	BRS Volume 86 Page 156
18 Parker, Peter	1610	St Michael Bassishaw	BRS Volume 89 Page 284
19 Porter, Thos	1643	St Ethelburga	BRS Volume 89 Page 301
20 Reve, Jn	1579	St Katherine Cree	BRS Volume 97 Page 356
21 Rolff, Rd	1456	St Peter Cornhill	BRS Volume 82 Page 157
22 Russell, Jn	1395	St Michael Cornhill	BRS Volume 89 Page 326
23 Styan, Tho	1552	St Botolph Bishopsgate	BRS Volume 86 Page 257
24 Whatley, Rd	1604	St Andrew Holborn	BRS Volume 89 Page 404
25 WilkinsonWm	1556	St Steven Coleman St	BRS Volume 86 Page 290
26 Wye, Wm	1641	Christchurch Newgate	BRS Volume 102 Page 762

The oft repeated statement that the Water-bearers "resided chiefly in Cobb's Court" has been discussed in Chapter 3. The map overleaf shows the Parish of residence for all except two of the Will makers, Nos 2 and 14, who lived in the parish of St Giles in the Fields to the west of the City. Cobb's Court is shown in the south west of the city between St Paul's Cathedral and the line of the old Roman Wall.

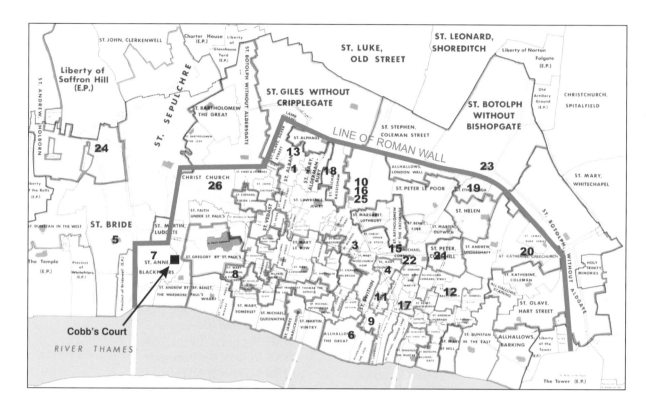

Parishes of residence of 24 Water-bearers who made Wills, 1394–1675. Prior to the Great Fire there were just over 100 Parishes in the square mile of the City. The original map, on which this is based, is intended largely for genealogical research and shows in colour the remarkable jig-saw of Parishes and Ecclesiastical Court Jurisdictions.

APPENDIX D

Admissions to the Fraternity 1632–1650

The figures tabulated below are taken from entries in the City Cash books, where they appear under the heading "Receipts Extraordinary"

Year	Freemen admitted @ 12d each	Foreigners admitted @ 2s-0d each	Total fines	Moiety paid to the City
1632	15	7	10s 0d	19s 6d
1633	33	13	10s 0d	34s 6d
1634	30	7	8s 0d	26s 0d
1635	28	4	7s 10d	21s 11d
1636	4	2	8s 0d	8s 0d
1637	16	2	6s 8d	13s 4d
1638	28	8	6s 0d	25s 0d
1639	21	2	6s 0d	15s 6d
1640	22	2	7s 0d	16s 6d
1641	25	2	5s 0d	17s 0d
1642/43	41		16s 0d	28s 6d
1644	5		8s 0d	6s 6d
1645	14		8s 0d	11s 0d
1646	21		8s 0d	14s 6d
1647	29		8s 0d	18s 6d
1648	34		6s 0d	20s 0d
1649	14		6s 0d	10s 0d
1650	12		8s 0d	10s 0d

APPENDIX E

The puzzle of Laroon's picture of a Water-bearer

Probably the best-known of all the pictures of Water-bearers in London is that by Marcellus Laroon, shown here. It was one of a series of 70 "Cries of London" which he produced in 1688. Because of the high quality of his pictures they all proved to be very popular and were reprinted and copied extensively in various series of "Cries" over a period of more than 50 years.

Laroon's picture of 1688

His image of a Water-bearer has since been reproduced, without comment, in many books and articles about early water supplies in London. As the present study has progressed it has, however, come to seem increasingly anomalous. It appears to be the only contemporary picture purporting to show a Water-bearer in London carrying a yoke and buckets.

The uniqueness of Laroon's image can be judged from seven other pictures reproduced in this book. Three of them show a single Water-bearer carrying a tankard – on pages 2, 22 and 30. In each of the pictures on pages 5 and 11 there is a tankard on the shoulder of a Water-bearer and another standing beside the Conduit. While enlarged parts of the pictures on pages 24 and 27, reproduced below, show fourteen and five tankards respectively: the latter also shows various buckets being used by housewives, one of whom possibly has a yoke.

Apart from these pictures, there is also the written word. The first record of a Water-bearer in 1276 refers to his having a tankard. The original Ordinances of the Fraternity in 1496 refer to tankards, as also do the City's rulings of 1562 amd 1680, and one additional Ordinance of 1556. None of these documents refers to the use of buckets by Water-bearers in the City of London. But, as already noted, the term "Tankard bearers" was quite frequently used to describe their trade.

The caption to Laroon's picture also poses a problem. The English version is "New River Water", while the French is "Qui veut de l'eau". In 1688 the New River Company was still engaged in its century-long endeavours to encourage more people to become customers for its piped water – in direct competition with that available from other sources – the Thames, wells, pumps and the Conduits, some of it distributed by Water-bearers. Although the New River Company was eventually asked to make water available to the Water-bearers while Aldersey was re-rerouting the principally aqueduct, that was not until 1693. It seems odd that the New River Company should, in 1688, have been selling its water via Water-bearers.

Marcellus Laroon was of Dutch origin, and it might be thought that perhaps he had taken his image from a Water-bearer in a Continental city. But he moved to England when he was quite young and at one time lived[265] in the Covent Garden area, so he should habitually have seen Water-bearers when he went into the City. His picture is an unexplained puzzle.

APPENDIX F

Water quality

The statement in Chapter 3 that "the quality of the New River water was probably also inferior" (as compared with the Conduit water) may cause surprise. The image of the New River being fed from clear, sparkling chalk springs in Hertfordshire is an enduring one: but it does not stand up to examination.

The chalk springs that were tapped initially at Amwell and Chadwell were doubtless clear and sparkling, but from the outset the water reaching the City was not by any means the same. The Company soon discovered that, for those living nearby, their 38 mile long canal-like watercourse provided an ideal repository for unwanted garbage of all descriptions[266]. In 1615 they complained of the:

> "... many abuses and misdemeanours daylie comitted and done, in and upon the said river, by lewde and ill-disposed people ... castinge in dogges and filth, and lettinge in sewers and other fowle and uncleane water, to the annoyance of the said water ..."

Although as many as 14 walksmen[267] were employed to patrol the banks regularly they could not entirely prevent these misdemeanours and the Company's Charter[268] of 1619 sought to prohibit people from:

> "... throwing or putting into the river anie earth, rubbish, soyle, gravell, stones, dogges, Catts or anie Cattle, Carrion, or anie unwholesome or uncleane thinge"

Two further provisions sought to forbid the washing of clothes in the river and allowing any "sincke, sewer, ditche, Tanhowse, dying howse" etc from draining into it.

The quality of the New River supply must have been further degraded when after only a few years – in 1620 – the quantity of the supply was augmented by tapping into the River Lee[269] at a point where it drained much of Hertfordshire, including the communities of Harpenden, Welwyn and Hertford.

At a much later date, in 1853, a pamphleteer by the name of Burch[270], who was opposing a further scheme to abstract more water from further down the River Lee described in colourful terms the quality problems of such open watercourses when no other method of rubbish disposal was generally available to the public. He complained that:

> *"The River Lee ... is the only means of getting rid of the sewage and*
> *filth of the towns, villages, etc which is considerable. It is, in fact, the*
> *sewer of the valley; all refuse is thrown or drained into it, and carried*
> *away by the stream; when dogs get mangey or cats get too old to*
> *catch mice, a stone is tied around their necks and they are bundled*
> *into the river. Numbers of dead bodies, canine and feline, float down*
> *in various stages of decay, diversified with an occasional calf, pig,*
> *dead fish, etc"*

For many years the water from the New River did not receive any serious treatment before being put into supply. There was a "grating"[271] at the point where the water from the Round Pond in Islington passed into a cistern feeding into the elm pipes, and the grosser impurities such as animal corpses were presumably scooped out there.

By comparison, the conduit supplies which were conveyed to the City in closed pipelines under positive pressure were probably of better overall quality, at least in the early years when the catchment areas west and north of the City were still predominantly rural.

But this advantage of the Conduit supplies was gradually eroded as the West End developed

Thus, when the condition of the City's headworks near Tyburn was thoroughly reported upon[272] in 1673 it was stated that "in the highway lies a great and noisome dunghill the issues of which sink into the City's Drains and very much prejudice the Water" And also "a drain is cut out of the highway into a field for the letting in of Ditch water to overflow it which (leaking in to the City's Drains made from the Round head through that field) very much discoloureth and dismayeth the City's Water. Which is also in great danger by the interment of Corpses too near thereunto". (The corpses were presumably from the nearby gallows, where up to 24 malefactors could be hung at one time: their bodies were afterwards thrown into pits nearby)[273].

Much later, when the science of water examination and analysis emerged during the second half of the 19th Century the facts about the New River supply became evident. Although, particularly from the viewpoint of public health, the New River water was nothing like so badly polluted as water from the River Thames, it was nevertheless far from pure. The early reports of Col Sir Francis Bolton and Professor Edward Frankland confirm that when the water reached London it was very different from the clear, sparkling water emerging from the springs in Hertfordshire.

In December 1871 the water arriving at the New River Company's works was described[274] as "turbid". By that time sand filtration had been installed, but even with that degree of treatment the water going into supply was still, on occasion, far from perfect even to the naked eye. In January 1877 the New River water, after filtration, was described[275] as "slightly turbid and very pale brown" and two months later it was an unsavoury "clear and very slightly yellow".

These descriptions refer to the water leaving the New River Company's works. Like every other piped supply at that time, the quality probably deteriorated further before it reached the customer. The maintenance of positive pressures constantly in water distribution systems – in order to ensure that all leakage is outward, and not inward – was not recognised as being important until quite late in the search for improved quality[276]. It was not enforced in London until the Metropolis Water Act of 1871.

APPENDIX G

The City's Aqueducts and Conduits

The City's Aqueducts and Conduits, which were commenced in 1237 and operated successfully for hundreds of years, would make an interesting study for some future engineering historian.

This account of the history of the Water-bearers has touched on a few aspects of the aqueducts, particularly on the failure in 1695 of the 5" dia lead pipe to deliver as much water to the Conduits in the City as expected. But no attempt has been made to explore the physical details of what were, in their day, very advanced – and expensive – items of public works.

The Corporation of London Record Office hold a wealth of documents relating to the early history of the City and further relevant facts about the Aqueducts – their design, construction and maintenance – could doubtless be found there, and probably in other repositories too, by a diligent searcher. A few pointers may be mentioned.

On several occasions the City Plumber was instructed by the Court of Aldermen to record details and prepare plans of the aqueducts, particularly the principal lines from Marylebone and Paddington, via Tyburn to the City. We have made no attempt to follow up these records, but have seen one 1/1440 plan dating from the 17th Century[277] which shows clearly a line of twin 3" dia lead pipes from Paddington to Tyburn, partly above and partly below ground, equipped at one point with an "air pipe". This suggests that the dangers of air locking (even with the leaky pipes then used) may have been understood in the design of this particular line. (It was not until much later, in the 19th Century, that the invention of automatic air valves for use at summits allowed greater freedom and economy in the choice of pressure pipeline depths).

Estimates of the natural contours around Tyburn, at the time when that area was still rural, are sketchy, but it seems possible that the stream which afforded the original supply may not have been any higher than the top of the cistern in each Conduit structure in the City. In other words, no valving on the aqueduct may have been needed to prevent overflowing and waste at the Conduits. The measurement by the City plumber in 1668 to establish[278] the height to which water could be raised at the East End of St Dunstan's Church seem to substantiate this suggestion. And although the measurements of level by Edmond Halley[279] in 1695 are not fully explicit they also seem to accord with this idea.

There are occasional references in later writings to the use of materials other than lead for the pipes – stoneware, timber and even leather – but it seems that lead was probably the material of choice. Its cost was evidently high, and Mr Aldersey's offer to replace the main conduit on a new alignment under public streets was clearly dependent on his being allowed to reclaim all the existing pipes. This was so important to him that soon after his contract had been finalised a separate document was drawn up confirming his right to take up the existing lead pipes[280]. Depending on the number and diameter of the existing pipelines it seems quite possible that he may have finished up with a surplus of lead.

A reference to the King seeking to borrow the City's "mould for the casting of a great water pipe" in 1551 shows[281] that the relatively new technique for casting lead pipe had by then been adopted by the City. It would be interesting to know what diameter qualified as "great" at that time. During the negotiations with Aldersey the Improvements Committee specified[282] that the diameter of his new 5 inch pipe should nowhere be less than 4¾ inches. This seems a large tolerance for a method of manufacture utilising a mandrel, and it would be interesting to know whether this was a generally recognised figure.

A Contractor's account of 1688 survives for carrying out 750 yards of trenching for the Aldgate Conduit. The account is reproduced opposite[283] and is of interest in illustrating the remarkable depths at which some of the supply pipes to the Conduits had to be laid, presumably because of higher ground intervening between the source and the Conduit. In this case, more than 300 yards of the trench was 15 feet deep and none of it was less than 10 feet deep, which must have added greatly to the expense of the work. The fact that the trench for the laying of a small pipe was no less than 4 feet wide is also noteworthy.

Ralph Treswell's map of 1585 (page 24) shows multiple pipes of the main aqueduct above ground in Cheapside. This is surprising when Cheapside was one of the most important streets in the City and, as recorded by Stow a few years later, there were increasing numbers of cars, drays, carts and coaches. The pipes were probably of lead and one would have thought the passage of hooves and wheels over them both inconvenient and damaging. However, the way in which one of the pipes branches into the Little Conduit, and a carefully measured gap in front of the church, seem to confirm that they were, indeed, above ground.

The "Banquetting House" near Tyburn, where the Lord Mayor presided over an annual feast celebrating the importance of the Conduit supplies, is mentioned repeatedly. An inventory of 1651 provides a useful list[284] of various cisterns, pumps and other water-related items both in the Banquetting House and in several other facilities associated with the Conduits.

The need for maintenance and repair was not overlooked. In Mr Aldersey's

The Ground Diged for the laying of the New Pipes, from the Tanter Ground neer Boll Lane, in the Spittle Fields, to Aldgate Coundite, Contains as followeth; viz.

Yards Solid

In 950 Foot Long, at 15 Foot Deepe, and 4 foot Broad, is containes Solid Yards —— 2 1 1 1

In 400 Foot Long, at 12 Foot Deepe, and 4 Foot Broad, is Containes Solid Yards —— 0 7 1 1

In 900 Foot Long, at Ten Foot Deepe and 4 Foot Broad, is Containes Solid Yards —— 1 3 3 3

Solid Yards in all 4 1 5 5

The which at Eight Pence ℈ Yard is —— 13 s . 10 . 00 ᵈ

Measured the 22ᵗʰ of March 168 7/8 .

℈ *Will. Leybourn.*

ſandby for the Watch —— 00 1 = 3 = 8
foure ſoldr & ſandby for ℈ plumd 00 2 = 2 = 3
————————
= 3 . 5 . 11

proposal[285] of 1692 for relaying the main supply pipe from Tyburn to the City he commented that although most of the length would be 3 or 4 feet in the ground, near Albermarle Buildings the height of the ground would make it necessary to provide 'a vault of brick so that breaches in the pipe may be mended there as well as in all other places'.

Over a period of more than 400 years prior to the Great Fire 15 Conduits had been established in the City from which Water-bearers and others could collect water free of charge, as listed below.

1. Fleet Conduit (1388)
2. Holborn Conduit (1498)
3. The little Conduit in West Cheap (c.1398)
4. Standard & Conduit in Cheapside (1395)
5. The Great Conduit (E end, Cheapside) (c.1245)
6. Stocks Market, the Pissing Conduit (1500)
7. Cornhill - the Tun near the pillory (1401)
8. Cornhill at Bishopsgate Street (1378)
9. Cripplegate (1438)
10. Aldermanbury (1471)
11. London Wall (Coleman Street) (1517)
12. Gracechurch Street (1491)
13. Bishopsgate (1505)
14. Aldgate Without (1535)
15. Lothbury (1546)

Most of these Conduit Structures were located in the middle of streets, the names of which are largely unchanged today, but the Standard and Conduit in Cheapside (No 4) was sometimes known by the name of nearby Honey Lane.

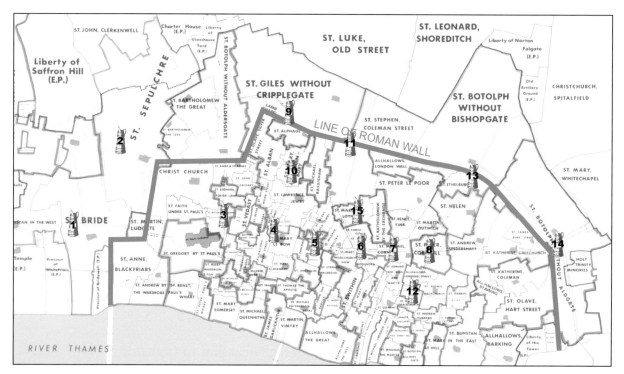

General distribution of Conduits in the City, as listed by number above.

Their general distribution in the central and northern parts of the City is shown opposite. The main aqueducts from Tyburn probably supplied the line of Conduits running through the centre of the City in Cheapside and Cornhill (Nos 3-8), plus Fleet Street (No 1), Aldermanbury (No10) and Gracious Street (12) (Gracechurch Street today). A 16th Conduit, known as Lamb's Conduit, was located well to the north-west of this area.

The exact locations of the 13 Conduits established by 1520 (Nos 1 to 13 on the list above) are shown on the excellent 1/2500 maps of the City of London published by Oxford University Press in 1989 in Volume III of the series "British Atlas of Historic Towns". Lambs's Conduit was sited at the north-east end of the present-day Lamb's Conduit Street.

At a late stage, markers were evidently installed to show the positions of the buried pipelines. When Samuel Pepys[286] was travelling with the Lord Mayor in his coach in September 1663 the latter pointed out to him "how the pillar set up by Exeter House is only to show where the pipes of Water run into the City".

Although the main Conduit supplies and the New River were gravitational, pumping was increasingly employed from the 16th Century onwards. Before the age of steam, various power sources were utilised, the most successful being Peter Morice's equipment making use of the rush of water through the arches of London Bridge. Manual pumping by the Water-bearers as a temporary expedient in 1621 has been described in Chapter 3. Pumps driven by windmills in Tottenham Court Road and the Strand are mentioned[287] and there were horse-driven pumps at Broken Wharf contrived by the mining engineer, Bevis Bulmer. These latter were eventually taken out of use 'on account of the great charge of working' them[288].

References

The sources of primary records quoted are abbreviated throughout as follows:
CLRO – Corporation of London Record Office, Guildhall
LMA – London Metropolitan Archives,
GLMR – Guildhall Library, Manuscripts Room

1. Foord A S, "Springs, streams and spas of London", T Fisher Unwin, 1910, p. 25.
2. Sharpe R, "Calendar of Letters of the City of London, Book A, c1275–1298", John Edward Francis, 1899, pp. 14 & 15.
3. Baker T, "Medieval London", Cassell, 1970, p. 247.
4. Barton N, "The lost rivers of London", Historical Publications Ltd, revised edition, 1994, pp. 105, 115 & 125–6.
5. Foord A S, "Springs, streams and spas of London", T Fisher Unwin, 1910, footnote 2, p. 253.
6. Stow J, "Survay of London", Routledge and Sons, 1893, pp. 48–50.
7. Stringer G F, "The Romance of London's Water Supply", The Morning Post, 9th December 1935, p. 7.
8. Dickinson H W, "Water Supply of Greater London", Newcomen Society, 1954, pp.16 & 17.
9. Gough J W, "Sir Hugh Myddelton", Clarendon Press, 1964, p.58.
10. Riley H T, "Memorials of London in the 13th, 14th and 15th Centuries", Longman Green & Co, 1868, p. 6.
11. Thomas A H, "Calendar of early Mayor's Court Rolls 1298–1309", Cambridge University Press, 1929, p.1.
12. Riley H T, "Memorials of London in the 13th, 14th and 15th Centuries", Longman Green & Co, 1868, p. 7.
13. Sharpe R, "Calendar of Letters of the City of London, Book F, 1337–1352", John Edward Francis, 1904, p. 215.

14. Sharpe R, "Calendar of Coroner's Rolls of the City of London, 1300–1378", Richard Clay and Sons, 1913, p. 106.
15. Unwin G, "The Gilds and Companies of London", 4th Edition, Frank Cass & Co, London, 1963, p. 81.
16. Sharpe R, "Calendar of Coroner's Rolls of the City of London, 1300–1378", Richard Clay and Sons, 1913, pp. 219 & 220.
17. Thomas A H, "Calendar of Plea and memoranda rolls of the City of London 1364–1381", Cambridge University Press, 1924, pp. 288 & 289.
18. Overall W H, "The accounts of the Churchwardens of the Parish of St Michael's Cornhill in the City of London from 1456 to 1608" A J Waterlow, c.1868, footnote 3, p. 219.
19. Daynes J N, "A short history of the Ancient Mistery of the Dyers of the City of London", Metcalfe and Cooper, 1965, p. 3.
20. Crewdson H A F, "Worshipful Company of Musicians", Charles Knight, 1971, p. 27.
21. Welch C, "History of the Worshipful Company of Pewterers of the City of London", Blades, East and Blades, 1902, p. iii.
22. Ridley J, "A History of the Carpenters Company", The Carpenters Company, 1995, p. 32.
23. Phillips F T, "A History of the Worshipful Company of Cooks", Worshipful Company of Cooks, 1932, p. 28.
24. "The Worshipful Company of Wax Chandlers", 2001, GL PAM 21933.
25. Coote H C, "The Ordinances of some secular Guilds of London 1354 to 1496, "Transactions of the London and Middlesex Archaeological Society", Vol IV Part 1, January 1871, p. 2 & 55–58: GLMR, London Commisssary Court Registers, Register of Wills, 1489–1502, Harvey MS 9171/8, fo 138 et seq.

26. Unwin G, "Gilds and Companies of London", 4th Edition, Frank Cass & Co, 1963, Chapter VIII, The Fraternities of Crafts

27. Ibid. p. 93.

28. Ibid. p. 217.

29. Ibid. p. 28.

30. Knowles D and Hadcock N, "Medieval Religious Houses – England and Wales", Longman, 1971, p. 242.

31. Hunting P, "The Garden House", MEPC, 1987, pp. 10–14.

32. Robertson A G, "Tudor London", Discovering London 4, Macdonald, 1968, pp. 73 & 74.

33. CLRO, Repertory 11, fo. 342.

34. CLRO, Repertory 13, fo. 63b.

35. CLRO, Journal 14, fo. 287b.

36. CLRO, Repertory 24, fo. 472b.

37. Hayes R, Historic Manuscripts Commission, Personal communication, 2003

38. Unwin G, "Gilds and Companies of London", 4th Edition, Frank Cass & Co, 1963, pp. 352 et seq.

39. Ibid. pp. 358–9.

40. CLRO, Repertory 13, fo. 162b.

41. CLRO, Repertory 13(2), fo. 299.

42. CLRO, Repertory 13(2), fos. 427b & 428.

43. CLRO, Repertory 15, fo. 16b.

44. Ibid. fo. 66b.

45. CLRO, Letter Book T, fo. 92.

46. Jenner M, Water in London 1500–1725, "Londinopolis", Manchester University Press, 2002, p. 260.

47. Unwin G, "Gilds and Companies of London", 4th Edition, Frank Cass & Co, 1963, p. 245.

48. Ibid. p. 251.

49. CLRO, Letter Book V, fo. 255.

50. Masters B, "Chamber accounts of the Sixteenth Century", London Record Society, Vol 20, 1984, p. 66.

51. CLRO, Repertory 24, fo. 467b.

52. CLRO, Repertory 53, fo. 110.

53 Ibid. fo. 213.

54. Ibid. fo. 117.

55. Overall W H, "The accounts of the Churchwardens of the Parish of St Michael's Cornhill in the City of London from 1456 to 1608", A J Waterlow, c.1868, p. 238.

56. "Law Reports, Equity Cases", 1870, Vol XI, Wm Clowes, pp. 35 et seq.

57. Coote H C, The Ordinances of some secular Guilds of London 1354 to 1496, "Transactions of the London and Middlesex Archaeological Society", Vol IV Part 1, January 1871, footnote, p. 58.

58. Jackson A A, "London Termini", 2nd Edition, 1985, David and Charles, p.110.

59. Stow J, "Survay of London", Routledge and Sons, 1893, p. 180.

60. CLRO, Letter Book V, fo. 255.

61. Unwin G, "Gilds and Companies of London", 4th Edition, Frank Cass & Co, 1963, pp 108 & 172.

62. Hunt W G, Windsor Herald of Arms, Personal Communication, April 2002.

63. Will of Sir James Cambell, PCC, Prob 1/88, 10/1/1642. In his Will this wealthy ironmonger left £5 to the wife of "Rogere, the Sexton, my old Waterbearer".

64. Clifford F, "History of Private Bill legislation", vol ii, Butterworth, 1887, p. 61.

65. Jonson B, "Every Man in His Humour", New Mermaid edition, 1998, p. 26.

66. Ibid. p. 4.

67. Unwin G, "Gilds and Companies of London", 4th Edition, Frank Cass & Co, 1963, p. 221.

68. LMA, Bridges c Stockdale, DL/C/214/ fo. 46.

69. Ibid. fo. 52.

70. Giese L I, "London Consistory Court Depositions 1586–1611", London Record Society, No 32, 1995, pp. 126, 127, 148, 149, 162 & 163.

71. LMA, Bridges c Stockdale, DL/C/214/ fo. 46.

72. Clifford F, "History of Private Bill legislation", vol ii, Butterworth, 1887, p. 61.

73. Masters B, "Chamber accounts of the Sixteenth Century", London Record Society, Vol 20, 1984, p. 66.

74. Ibid. p. 8.

75. CLRO, Chamber accounts 16th Century Vol 1, fo. 126.

76. CLRO, City Cash 1/1 to 1/7.

77. Will of Thomas Hartopp, PCC, Register Tirwhite, 5/11/1582. A further provision of Thomas Hartopp's Will referred to Hugh Myddelton, who was evidently apprenticed to him.

78. Coote H C, "The Ordinances of some secular Guilds of London 1354 to 1496, "Transactions of the London and Middlesex Archaeological Society", Vol IV, Part 1, January 1871, p.56 & para 10, Appendix A.

79. Jonson B, "Every Man in His Humour", New Mermaid edition, 1998, p. 27.

80. GLMR, "St Martins Ludgate Vestry Minutes Book 1568–1649 Part I", fo. 66.

81. CLRO, Repertory 26 (1), fo.144b.

82. CLRO, Journal 49, fo. 142 (Appendix B line 216).

83. CLRO, Repertory 59, fo. 363 & 363b.

84. Sharpe R, "Calendar of Letters of the City of London, Book I, 1400–1422", John Edward Francis, 1909, p.178.

85. Clifford F, "History of Private Bill legislation", vol ii, Butterworth, 1887, p. 61.

86. CLRO, Letter Book V, fo. 255.

87. CLRO, Journal 49, fo. 142 (Appendix B, line 206).

88. Perrin R, Personal Communication, February 2003

89. CLRO, Repertory 44, fo. 137b.

90. Laroon M, "Cries of London", 1688, GL closed access A.5.2.N030

91. Barton N, "The lost rivers of London", Historical Publications Ltd, revised edition, 1994, p. 83.

92. Darlington I, "The London Commissioners of Sewers and their Records", Phillimore, 1970, p. 34.

93 Riley H T, "Memorials of London in the 13th, 14th and 15th Centuries", Longman Green & Co, 1868, p. 7, note 2.

94. Hodgett G A J, "The Cartulary of Holy Trinity Aldgate", London Record Society, No7, 1970, pp 183, 185–186 & 189.

95. Sharpe R, "Calendar of Wills proved and enrolled in the Court of Husting, London, Part I, 1258–1358", John C Francis, 1889, pp. 509 and 559.

96. Riley H T, "Memorials of London in the 13th, 14th and 15th Centuries", Longman, Green & Co, 1868, page 254.

97. Sharpe R, "Calendar of Letters of the City of London, Book G, 1352–1374", John Edward Francis, 1905, p. 206.

98. Clifford F, "History of Private Bill Legislation", Butterworth, 1887, vol ii, p. 44.

99. Jonson B, "Every Man in His Humour", New Mermaid Edition, 1998, pp XXVII–XXIX.

100. CLRO, Repertory 64, fo. 167b.

101 Antiquary A London, Memoirs of William Lamb, "Gentlemen's Magazine", 53, 1783, part I, p.135.

102. CLRO, Journal 14, fo. 287b.

103. Sharpe R, "Calendar of Letters of the City of London, Book F, 1337–1352", John Edward Francis, 1904, p.123.

104. Stow J, "Survay of London", Routledge and Sons, 1893, p.110.

105. Kingsford C L, "Chronicles of London", Clarendon Press, 1905, pp.301–303 & 333.

106. Clifford F, "History of Private Bill Legislation", Butterworth, 1887, vol ii, p. 37 footnote 4.

107. CLRO, Repertory 118, fo. 377.

108. Memoir of William Lamb, "Gentlemen's Magazine", 53, 1783, part I, p.137.

109. Latham R and Matthews W, "The Diary of Samuel Pepys", University of California Press, Vol 1, p. 3 and Note 2.

110. CLRO, Repertory 20, fo 425b.

111. CLRO, Repertory 8, fo. 66b.

112. Sharpe R, "Calendar of Letters of the City of London, Book I, 1400–1422", John Edward Francis, 1909, p.139, note 2.

113. Schofield, J "Medieval London Houses", Paul Mellon Centre, 1994, page 233.

114. Barty-King H, "Water", 1992, p. 36.

115. CLRO, Journal 14, fo. 287b.

116. CLRO, Repertory 15, fo. 38b.

117. Sharpe R, "Calendar of Letters of the City of London, Book D, 1309–1314", John Edward Francis, 1902, pp.236 & 237.

118. Sharpe R, "Calendar of Letters of the City of London, Book I, 1400–1422", John Edward Francis, 1909, p.139.

119. CLRO, Repertory 74, fo. 228b.

120. Jenner M, Water in London 1500–1725, "Londinopolis", Manchester University Press, 2002, p. 250.

121. Cook D, Personal Communication, July 2003. Cobham House had once been the guest house of Blackfriars Priory. The garden, presumably for growing medicinal herbs as well as for recreational use and meditation, had been maintained by the Howard family to whom the property had belonged after the Reformation until it was purchased by the Society of Apothecaries.

122. Parsloe G, "Wardens Accounts of the Worshipful Company of Founders in the City of London 1497–1681", Athlone Press, 1964, p. 6.

123. Littlehales H,"The Medieval Records of a London City Church – Mary at Hill", Early English Text Society, Original Series 125 &128, London, 1905, pp. 328 & 343.

124. Sharpe R, "Calendar of Letters of the City of London, Book E, 1314–1337", John Edward Francis, 1903, p. 204.

125. CLRO, Repertory 26 (1), fo.144b.

126. Sharpe R, "Calendar of Letters of the City of London, Book F, 1337–1352", John Edward Francis, 1904, pp. 28 & 29.

127. Seaver P, "Wallington's World", Methuen, 1985, pp. 53 & 54.

128. CLRO, Repertory 36, fo. 231.

129. CLRO, City Cash 1/8, fo. 7.

130. Clifford F, "History of Private Bill legislation," vol ii, Butterworth, 1887, pp. 61–64.

131. Keble J, "The Statutes at Large in paragraphs from Magna Carta until this time", Bill, Baker and Atkins, 1676, pp. 596–598.

132. CLRO, Journal 14, fo. 30b.

133. CLRO, Remembrancia II, fo. 321.

134. CLRO, Repertory 14, fos. 519, 520b & 523.

135. CLRO, Repertory 30, fos. 258, 262 & 262b.

136. CLRO, Repertory 31 (1), fos 83b & 129.

137. CLRO, Repertory 34, fo. 473b.

138. CLRO, Repertory 31 (2), fo. 342.

139. Sharpe R, "Calendar of Letters of the City of London, Book H, 1375–1399", John Edward Francis, 1907, p. 326.

140. CLRO, Journal 8, fo. 184b & 185.

141. "Loyal London Mercury or the current intelligence", No 16, 11–14, October 1682, front page.

142. Nichols J G, "The diary of Henry Machyn, Citizen and Merchant Taylor of London 1550–1563", Camden Society, 1848, p. 245–246.

143. CLRO, Remembrancia I, fo 222v.

144. Dickinson H W, "Water Supply of Greater London", Newcomen Society, 1954, p. 14.

145. CLRO, Repertory 12 (2), fo 408.

146. Foord A S, "Springs, streams and spas of London", T Fisher Unwin, 1910, p. 311.

147. Gough J W, "Sir Hugh Myddelton", Clarendon Press, 1964, p.66 footnote.

148. Stringer G F, "The Romance of London's Water Supply", The Morning Post, 9th December 1935, p. 5: Gough J W, "Sir Hugh Myddelton", Clarendon Press, 1964, p. 58.

149. Berry G C, "Sir Hugh Myddelton and the New River", lecture delivered to the Honourable Society of Cymmrodorion, 1956, pp. 39 & 40.

150. Gough J W, "Sir Hugh Myddelton", Clarendon Press, 1964, p. 62.

151. Berry G C, "Sir Hugh Myddelton and the New River", lecture delivered to the Honourable Society of Cymmrodorion, 1956, p. 39 & 40.

152. Gough J W, "Sir Hugh Myddelton", Clarendon Press, 1964, p. 62 footnote.

153. Berry G C, "Sir Hugh Myddelton and the New River", lecture delivered to the Honourable Society of Cymmrodorion, 1956, p. 41.

154. Inwood S, "History of London", Macmillan, 1998, p. 281.

155. Institution of Water Engineers, "The Manual of British Water Supply Practice", Second Edition, 1954, W Heffer & Sons, p.9.

156. Darlington I, "The London Commissioners of Sewers and their Records", Phillimore, 1970, p. 39.

157. Gough J W, "Sir Hugh Myddelton", Clarendon Press, 1964, p. 63.

158. Bolton F, "Reports of the examination during months of 1874–1880 of the water supplied by the Metropolitan Water Companies before and after filtration at the works", The Local Government Board

159. Richardson J, "London and its People", Barrie and Jenkins, 1995, p. 73.

160. CLRO, Repertory 104, fo. 287.

161. GLMR, St Martins Ludgate Vestry Minutes Book 1568–1649 Part 1, fo. 66.

162. Cook D, Personal Communication, July 2003

163. Seaver P, "Wallington's World", Methuen, 1985, p. 54.

164. Munby L, "How much is that worth?", British Association for Local History, Phillimore, second edition, 1996, p.38.

165. Clifford F, "History of Private Bill legislation", vol ii, Butterworth, 1887, p. 59 footnote: CLRO, Letter Book Q, fo 184v.

166. CLRO, Repertory 34, fo. 457b.

167. Derwent K, "Medieval London", Discovering London 3, Macdonald, 1968, p. 36.

168. Tomalin C, "Samuel Pepys – the unequalled self", Penguin Books, 2003, p. 5.

169. Milne G, "The Great Fire of London", Historical Publications Ltd, 1986, p. 10 & 79.

170. Porter S, "The Great Fire of London", Sutton Publishing Ltd, 1996, pp. 21 & 22.

171. Ibid. pp. 22 & 23

172. Prideaux, "Memorials of the Goldsmiths Company", Vol 2, Eyre & Spottiswoode, 1896, pp 71, 75 & 80.

173. Bell W G, "The Great Fire of London", Bodley Head, 1920, Appendix IV, page 338

174. Ibid. p. 60.

175. Ibid. p 35.

176. Inwood S, "History of London", Macmillan, 1998, p. 245.

177. Rolles S, "Shilhavtiyah or The Burning of London in the year 1666: commemorated and improved in a CX discourses, meditations and contemplations", London 1667, pp.153 et seq Meditation XL.

178. Latham R & Matthews W, "The Diary of Samuel Pepys", University of California Press, Vol X Companion, 1983, p. 331.

179. "The Statutes at Large from the 1st Year of King James the first to the tenth year of King William the third", Volume 3, pp. 303 et seq.

180. CLRO, Journal 46, fo. 238.

181. Ibid. fos. 252b, 253 & 253b.

182. CLRO, Repertory 80, fos. 205 & 205b.

183. CLRO, MS 359 (ex GL), two unfoliated.

184. CLRO, Journal 47, fo. 146b.

185. CLRO, Journal 48, fos 20 & 172.

186. CLRO, Journal 49, fos. 140 et seq (transcribed in Appendix B).

187. Ibid. fo. 100b.

188. CLRO, City Lands Vol E, fos. 59 & 60.

189. CLRO, Repertory 75, fo 31.

190. CLRO, Misc MSS/152/4, unfoliated.

191. CLRO, Repertory 86, fo. 42b.

192. Ibid. fo. 41.

193. CLRO, Repertory 87, fo. 40.

194. ibid. fo. 118b.

195. CLRO, Repertory 90, fo. 3b et seq.

196. CLRO, Repertory 92, fo. 255.

197. CLRO, Repertory 103, fo.161 & 162.

198. CLRO, Journal 54, fo. 651.

199. Foord A S, "Springs, streams and spas of London", T Fisher Unwin, 1910, p. 256.

200. CLRO, Repertory 78, fo 145b.

201. Ibid. fo. 272b.

202. Ibid. fos.157b &158.

203. CLRO, Repertory 81, fo 252.

204. CLRO Misc MSS/152/4, unfoliated.

205. CLRO, Repertory 81, fo 175.

206. CLRO, Repertory 90, fo.102.

207. CLRO, Journal 47, fo. 138b: also Repertory 76 fo. 245.

208. CLRO, Misc MSS/152/4, unfoliated.
209. CLRO, Misc MSS/152/4, unfoliated.
210. CLRO, Improvements Committee, 1692–94, fo. 5.
211. CLRO, Journal 51, fo. 214.
212. CLRO, Repertory 97, fo. 263.
213. Ibid. fo. 322.
214. Rudden B, "The New River – a legal history", Clarendon Press, 1985, p. 98.
215. CLRO, Journal 51, fos. 303b et seq.
216. CLRO, City Cash 1/21, fo. 123.
217. CLRO, Journal 51, fo. 214.
218. Ibid. fo. 304.
219. CLRO, Journal 52, fo. 76b: CLRO, Improvements Committee, 1692–94, fo. 182.
220. CLRO, Rep 99 (1), fo. 529.
221. CLRO, Misc MSS/371/4
222. CLRO, Journal 52, fo 80b Alderman Sir James Houblon (a close friend of Samuel Pepys) was appointed by the City Corporation. When he and the other arbitrator – appointed by Robert Aldersey – failed to agree on an award they jointly nominated Brooke Bridges Esq, Auditor to the Exchequer, as sole arbitrator. But after several meetings he expressed himself unwilling to determine the matter.
223. CLRO, Journal 52, fo. 322b et seq.
224. "English Report", Vol 23, 2 Vern 421, pp. 870 & 871; Vol 24, Proc Ch 156, p. 75; Vol 1 1 Bro P C, 516, pp. 727 & 728.
225. CLRO, Orphans 2nd Cash Book, 1692, fo 152v
226. CLRO, Journal 52, fos. 352b & 353.
227. GLMR, Court Minute Books, Wax Chandlers, 1584–1924, Ref 9485
228. CLRO, City Lands Deed 39.8.
229. CLRO, Journal 68, fo. 267 et seq.
230. CLRO, Repertories Indexes, Nos 97–154 (1692–1750) and Nos 155–203 (1751–1799)
231. CLRO, City Cash 1/15, fo 127.
232. CLRO, City Cash 1/18, fo 45.
233. CLRO, Journal 57, fos. 234b et seq.
234. CLRO, City Cash 1/7, fo 13: City Cash 2/35, fo. 45 & 125.
235. CLRO, City Cash 2/37, fo 47b.
236. Archer I, The Livery Companies and Charity during the Sixteenth and Seventeenth Centuries, "Guilds, Society and Economy in London 1450–1800", 2002, Centre for Metropolitan History, pp.23–25.
237. Stanton Ironworks Company, "Cast iron pipe: its life and service", Stanton, 1936, pp. 68 et seq.
238. Maitland W, "History of London", Richardson, 1739, p. 450.
239. Memoir of William Lamb, "Gentlemen's Magazine", 53, 1783, part I, p.135.
240. Clifford F,. "History of Private Bill legislation", vol ii, Butterworth, 1887, p. 78.
241. Mayhew, H, "London Characters and Crooks", Kimber, 1851, pp.70 & 71.
242. Gough J W, "Sir Hugh Myddelton", Clarendon Press, 1964, pp. 65 & 66.
243. Grimwade A, "London Silversmiths, 1697 to 1837", Faber, 1976, pp.502 & 503.
244. 1841 Census, HO107/688, Book 13, fo 22–24, 11, Paradise Row, Chelsea.
245. Death Certificate of William Eley, Registration District St George's Hanover Square, Sub District Mayfair, No 69, 25th June 1841.
246. Report under heading "Dreadful explosion in Old Bond Street", "The Times", 28th June, 1841.
247. Coroner's report of inquest held at Red Horse, Old Bond Street on 26th June 1841.
248. Death Certificate of Susannah Eley, Registration District Hampstead, No 439, 2nd September,1854
249. Snow J, "On the Mode of Transmission of Cholera", p. 44.
250. Burman J, "Chronicle of the World", Longman, 1989, p. 389.
251. Sharpe R, "Calendar of Letters of the City of London, Book G, 1352–1374", John Edward Francis, 1905, p.92.
252. The New Encyclopaedia Britannica, "Macropaedia", Vol 16, 15th Edition, 1993, pp. 605–610.
253. Horne G and Foord E, "Medieval London", Ernest Benn Ltd, 1927, pp.150–155
254. Archer I, "The pursuit of stability",

Cambridge University Press, 1991, pp. 2–4.

255. CLRO, Repertory 34, fo. 473b.

256. Unwin G, "Gilds and Companies of London," 4th Edition, Frank Cass & Co,1963, pp 166, 370–371

257 Clark A, "The Donkeys", Hutchinson, 1961.

258. Terraine J, "The Smoke and the Fire: myths and anti-myths of war, 1861–1945", Sidgwick and Jackson, 1982, pp. 170 et seq.

259. Overall W H, "The accounts of the Churchwardens of the Parish of St Michael's Cornhill in the City of London from 1456 to 1608", A J Waterlow, c.1868, footnote 3, p. 219.

260. Harben H A, "A Dictionary of London", Jenkins, 1918, p.613.

261. Harrison M, "London beneath the pavement", Peter Davis, 1971, p. 59.

262. "The Water Supply of London", Metropolitan Water Board, 1961, p. 2.

263. Barty-King H, "Water", 1992, p. 36.

264. "Index to Wills proved in the Prerogative Court of Canterbury, 1676–1700". British Record Society, Nos 71, 77 and 80, 1948, 1958 and 1960.

265. "Dictionary of National Biography", Vol XI, 1973, pp 594 et seq.

266. Gough J W, "Sir Hugh Myddelton", Clarendon Press, 1964, p. 67.

267. Maitland, "History of London", Richardson, 1739, p. 628.

268 Gough J W, "Sir Hugh Myddelton", Clarendon Press, 1964, p. 67.

269. Ibid. p. 74.

270. Burch W, "A practical essay on water supplies to the Metropois", Effingham Wilson, 1853, GL Pamphlet 4567, pp. 20 & 21.

271. Gough J W, "Sir Hugh Myddelton", Clarendon Press, 1964, p. 60.

272. CLRO, Repertory 78, fo. 146 & 146b.

273. Rumbelow D, "The Triple Tree - Newgate, Tyburn and Old Bailey", 1982, Harrap, p.160.

274. Bolton F, "Water Supply (Metropolis)

Copy of Reports to the Board of Trade made by the Water Examiner appointed under the Metropolis Water Act 1871", Ordered by the House of Commons to be printed 5 March 1872, p. 2.

275. "An examination of the figures and statements published as the result of the Analyses by Professor Frankland of the Metropolitan Water Supply in 1876 and 1877" 1878, Simpkin Marshall & Co, Table P.

276. "Public General Acts", 1871, Chapter 113, page 420, Sections 7 to 16.

277. CLRO, Surveyor City London, Plan No 1274, "Plan of the drains, openings, conduits, pipes from spring head at Paddington to receipt conduit", c 17th C, 1/1440.

278. CLRO, Journal 46, fo. 253.

279. CLRO, Misc MSS/371/4.

280. CLRO, Repertory 97, fo. 351.

281. CLRO, Repertory 12 (2), fo. 408

282. CLRO, Improvements Committee, 1692–94, fo. 48.

283. CLRO, Misc MSS/152/4.

284. CLRO, City Cash 1/8, fo 6b et seq.

285. CLRO, Journal 51, fo. 214.

286. Latham R and Matthews W, "The Diary of Samuel Pepys", University of California Press, Vol IV (1663), p.3.

287. Maitland W, "History of London", Richardson, 1739, pp 167 & 628.

288. Ibid. p. 167.

Index